STUDIES IN FRENCH LITERATURE

IX

THE CRITICAL RECEPTION

OF

GUSTAVE FLAUBERT

IN THE

UNITED STATES

1860 - 1960

by

ERNEST JACKSON

University of Hawaii

1966

MOUTON & CO.

THE HAGUE · PARIS

Printed in The Netherlands by Mouton & Co., Printers, The Hague

PREFACE

Gustave Flaubert is well known in the United States as the author of *Madame Bovary* and as the inventor of the modern realistic novel. Very little more is known of the impact which he has had upon the history of American fiction. The aim of this study is to define and clarify Flaubert's role in American novel writing by examining his critical reception in the United States, for it would seem that there is a great deal more to be learned than what has already been done about the critical attitudes toward Flaubert in this country during the approximately one hundred years that he has been known here. It is a generally accepted opinion that Zola, who had influenced Norris, Crane, Dreiser, and others, was the most important source of influence from the French naturalistic group which included Flaubert. Credit is paid to Flaubert for his creation of the realistic novel in *Madame Bovary*, and the work is cited as an historical landmark in the development of the realistic novel, but little more attention is paid to him.

The realistic novel in America today, with a few sensational exceptions, does not resemble the novel as created by Zola. In many cases, however, it does conform to those standards established by Flaubert while writing *Madame Bovary*. This conformity leads one to suspect that Flaubert's importance in America was more decisive and pervasive than is generally thought. It would seem, moreover, that his pre-eminence here was enduring.

The most important source of material for this study has been the critical notices in literary magazines and scholarly journals which have appeared over a period of one hundred years. Books about Flaubert and about criticism in general have also been utilized. The libraries of the University of Michigan and of the University of Hawaii have provided a complete coverage of the magazines and journals.

The study of Flaubert's critical reception has necessitated a brief review of his life, works, and literary ideals. A rapid survey of the development of American literary criticism has also proved helpful. The fortunes of Flaubert's works in this country have been inextricably linked with the changing critical standards and literary movements here. Both American criticism and the understanding that we have of Flaubert's writings have benefited from the relationship.

The bibliography includes all books and articles used in preparation of the study. Articles and some books used as primary sources are listed chronologically and numbered in Appendix A. Reference is made to them by number in the footnotes. Chronological lists of the English translations of Flaubert's works published in America and Ph. D. dissertations about Flaubert presented at American universities are given in Appendices B and C. The Index includes critics who have written articles about Flaubert published in American journals and periodicals and used in this study of his reception here.

This study was first presented as a doctoral dissertation at the University of Michigan. Grateful thanks are due to the members of the doctoral committee: Dr. Joe Lee Davis, Professor of English; Dr. James C. O'Neill, Professor of French; Dr. Monroe Z. Hafter, Assistant Professor of Spanish, who read the thesis and made helpful suggestions for revision and correction, and to Mrs. Mildred Knowlton, Honolulu, Hawaii, who gave much help with typing and checking foot notes and sources.

Special thanks are owed to Dr. Paul M. Spurlin, Professor of French, who suggested the subject. Over a long period of time he has read and re-read these pages making important suggestions for this final form which they have taken. His thoughtful and tolerant assistance has made the completion of this study possible.

TABLE OF CONTENTS

I

INTRODUCTION

Within the last ten years there has been a surprising increase in the appearance of Flaubert's name in American literary magazines and journals. New editions of his long-familiar works have been published. In the last decade seven editions of *Madame Bovary* have appeared, making a total of at least forty-four American editions of the novel since it first appeared here in translation in 1881. *Salammbô* has appeared once in this time and *L'Education sentimentale* has had three editions. His correspondence has been recently republished, in addition to new translations of those stories which had previously been known only through articles and literary discussions. Two editions of the *Dictionnaire des Idées reçues* and one of *Bouvard et Pécuchet* are now available.

Flaubert is known universally as the father of the realistic novel, a representative of the nineteenth century whose books are interesting historically and artistically, but who supposedly has enjoyed very little general public appreciation here. In reality, the interest in Flaubert on the part of the critics and the general public has continued steadily and undiminished from the time of the publication of his first novel in the United States. *Madame Bovary* is included in the list of best-selling books in America compiled by F. L. Mott.[1] The casual reader may be somewhat surprised to find this novel among the titles which we automatically accept as having captured the fancy of the American reading public. Mott estimated over a decade ago that the sales of this book had reached the million mark in America, or come close to it.[2]

[1] Frank Luther Mott, *Golden Multitudes* (New York, MacMillan Co., 1947), p. 310.
[2] *Ibid.*, p. 248.

In spite of this record, it is the assumption on the part of many students of literature that Flaubert is a "writer's writer" and not one who appeals to a general American reading public. His works are often treated solely as models for writers and critics. Because of this attitude, perhaps, there has been no lack of articles and books about the literary aspects of his novels and the impact that they have had on several generations of American writers and critics. These articles have appeared in a small but steady stream since the latter decades of the nineteenth century. They have not been carefully or precisely documented studies, for the most part, but they have been, almost uniformly, heated personal evaluations of the good or harm that Flaubert has done to American letters.

Since the latter part of the nineteenth century Flaubert has been hailed as the creator of the realistic novel and even as the father of the modern novel as a genre. *Madame Bovary* is a familiar name to nearly all literate Americans. There are not many serious students of American or European literature who have not at least heard of *L'Education sentimentale* and *Bouvard et Pécuchet*. Flaubert's influence on the form and technique of the novel has indeed become a commonplace in literary history.

Alfred Kazin has noted the appearance of the recent editions of Flaubert's works and the resurgence of articles about him. In his essay, "The Anger of Flaubert", in *The Inmost Leaf*, he has been led to ask:

Why is it that at a certain moment some writer from out of the past, some acknowledged classic whose greatness and permanent value have been taken for granted, who is a part of the history of the race and a symbol for certain virtues, unexpectedly becomes important to us? It is never his art as such that first sends us back to him, for art is always wrapped around a point of view, it is always some particular angle of vision, some blunt prejudice about life, the very tone of a man's voice, to which we are attracted again. Suddenly it is Flaubert to whom we instinctively respond, who brings out something for us that badly needs saying, and who, after having given his whole life to a particular vision, reappears before us as a hero.[3]

The question posed here by Kazin is a legitimate one. He intimates that the answer is sociological. This may be in part correct. There are

[3] New York, The Noonday Press, 1959, p. 109.

also those who would seek the answer in other directions. For the question seems too large to have a simple and limited response.

Flaubert has produced works which are today accepted in the United States as classics. Many classics of other novelists have fallen into neglect. This is not the case with Flaubert's works. We are led to ask, therefore, why their popularity has continued relatively strong. Waves of interest generated by the public are indicated by the numerous publications of his works at varying periods. Articles in literary reviews and journals show this same continuous interest on the part of the critics. Since it is impossible to interview readers from the general public of the past, and because the ordinary reader is not prone to leave a written testimonial concerning the books he has read, the chief source for finding the reasons for Flaubert's nearly continuous impact on American readers and writers is the body of critical writing which abounds. From an examination of this writing it may be ascertained if it is the intrinsic moral and artistic value of his works which accounts for their survival over the years or if the social, political, and economic conditions in the United States during certain eras have determined the establishment of Flaubert's works as masterpieces and fixed the level of their acceptance, or whether it is a combination of factors which may be counted.

The role of the critic is also involved here. In the case of Flaubert, who has set forth in his correspondence a credo of literary ideals and criteria and demonstrated their application in his works, an examination of the interactive role of the critic and the literature studied by him is most revealing. Interesting insights into both the function of the critic and the subject of his criticism are provided. And definite views as to the importance and the influence of artistic criteria and social attitudes emerge.

Flaubert is a prime subject for the study of the critical reception accorded a foreign author in the United States. His position as a master craftsman in the art of novel writing is unassailable. His opinions are definite and of far-reaching importance. Because of his fame and lofty position in the novelistic field, there is perhaps not a single major American writer or critic who has not felt in some measure the impact of Flaubert's ideals. Most of them have reacted in definite, though not in similar, ways. And today the American critic has come of age. He represents many and varied viewpoints. His influence is felt in many literatures. Flaubert has offered fruitful material for these divergent and influential attitudes. The American critical opinions about him have been numerous and rich in diversity throughout the years that he has been considered a major writer. Often in these differing viewpoints concerning Flaubert may be seen the changing values and attitudes which have appeared in the growth and development of American criticism. In addition, this American criticism has served the very useful purpose of shedding new light upon Flaubert and his worth as a writer.

Flaubert has enjoyed growing prestige in the United States since the last decade of the nineteenth century. His influence has been acknowledged by writer and critic alike, if not by the literary historian. But despite the many articles, essays, and occasional pieces, no effort has been made to trace with any precision the growth of his importance and the evolution of his impact upon the American literary scene by a study of American attitudes toward his works as evinced in critical writing. Studies of his influence on the English novel have been made[4] and Ernst von Helms Frienmuth has analyzed the German criticism of Flaubert[5] but no comparable study has been done here. On the other hand, Zola is often credited with being the major French influence on realism in this country. This is due perhaps to the fact that a definite influence from his works is more easily traceable in certain American authors. Zola's importance has been underlined by the fine studies of Frierson and Edwards[6] and Salvan.[7] The problem, however, is different in Flaubert's case. Flaubert today is generally accepted as the father of modern realistic writing by many American critics and even by historians of literature. Many prominent writers acknowledge their debt to him without being specific. And his impact on realism has patently

---

[4] Edward Conn, "The Impact of *Madame Bovary* on the English Novel". Unpublished Ph. D. thesis, Columbia University (1952). See also W. D. Ferguson, "The Influence of Flaubert on George Moore". Unpublished Ph. D. thesis, University of Pennsylvania (1934).

[5] *German Criticism of Gustave Flaubert* (New York, Columbia University Press, 1939).

[6] W. C. Frierson and H. Edwards, "Impact of French Naturalism on American Critical Opinion", *PMLA*, LXIII (1948), p. 1009.

[7] A. F. Salvan, *Zola aux Etats-Unis* (Providence, Brown University Press, 1943).

been so pervasive and wide that single traits in single authors are impossible to find.

Realism as practiced in American literature has a variety of characteristics. There are many possible definitions of the movement.[8] George Becker has formulated a satisfactory definition which attempts to include the three most important aspects of the school as it is practiced in America today.[9] First and most important is the realism of method. Becker finds that no precise technique has been established by which a writer may obtain the faithful and complete rendition of reality which is required by realism, but in general the practice of this type of writing is governed by three basic concepts. The author must place a great reliance upon documentation and observation. He must attempt to approximate the norm of experience. He must preserve the ideal of objectivity.

The second important aspect necessary for the achievement of a realistic literary work is realism of subject matter. The early realists treated man in society conceived as a simple environment. The viewpoint held by these innovators has been extended to the point where man is now viewed in an enlarged social complex. Added to the material manifestations of man's surroundings is the exploration of his physiological and psychological levels of existence. In order to avoid sensationalism or pedestrian collections of data these investigations must be controlled by the realistic method.

The final important aspect of modern realism is the philosophical base upon which it rests. In spite of the desired objectivity of the realists, it is impossible for them not to pass at least implicit judgment upon man and his fate.

In his article Becker underlines the confusion between realism and naturalism. He writes that the latter is often mistakenly identified with stark realism. Instead, naturalism is a philosophic extension of realism. Becker writes that "naturalism insists upon the existence of limitations to the efficacy of human personality and endeavor, and it places the boundaries of those limitations rather close at hand. It sees in the

---

[8]   See H. Levin, "What is Realism?", *Comparative Literature*, III (1951), pp. 193-199, for a perspective of changing viewpoints in the history of realism.
[9]   "Realism: An Essay in Definition", *Modern Language Quarterly*, X (1949), pp. 184-197.

activities of the consciousness little more than the efforts of an organism at adaptation, certainly in no sense the aspirations of the spirit toward identity with already existent Platonic ideals." [10]

It is necessary also to understand the climate of critical opinion in America during the period under consideration, from approximately 1860 to the present, in order to discover what were the criteria of good novels and the literary ideals of the American critics. Taine's theory of "la race, le moment et le milieu" still has a valid application in literary criticism. This is very true in America where such important books as Parrington's *The Beginnings of Critical Realism in America* have utilized this critical approach and influenced the trends of critical thought.[11] Flaubert certainly would not have been accepted in America if society were not disposed to receive him. But despite the predisposition of some of the critics and the reading public to accept new standards, their newly developed critical inclinations might well have remained in a vague and formless condition. An author who satisfies newly felt requirements may help formulate or crystallize critical opinion by means of his literary dicta and his works which illustrate them. An analysis of Flaubert criticism here will reveal whether or not this was the case with his writings.

The source material used here is limited to an examination of literary magazines such as *Harpers, Atlantic Monthly, Dial,* and many others. In addition, all of the scholarly journals relating to French and American literature are utilized. Outstanding and important books relating to American literary history, literary criticism, and to the social and economic forces in literature have also been examined. To evaluate the mass of material, pertinent background information concerning Flaubert is likewise indicated. A brief outline of his life with an exposition of his literary theories will afford a basis for evaluating and understanding the criticism as it appeared in America and will add to the comprehension of what he offered American readers that was peculiar to him and fulfilled a need here.

In the continuous stream of critical material about Flaubert which has appeared in this country there are indications of the changing climate of critical opinion. The great difference of subject matter in

---

[10] *Ibid.*, p. 193.
[11] New York, Harcourt, Brace and Co., 1931.

Flaubert's novels has been one of the causes for the divergent critical attitudes and viewpoints which have existed side by side for years. *Madame Bovary* has a typically realistic subject and receives realistic treatment. *Salammbô*, on the other hand, treats a subject and a period which are removed from nineteenth century reality and which are easily adapted to a romantic treatment. *La Tentation de Saint Antoine* is a literary tableau which is almost unique in its realistic subject and background; its treatment was completely novel for its time. *Bouvard et Pécuchet* is in a class by itself, but the book was inspired by the same sociological sentiments as was *L'Education sentimentale*. The strong link between these works is the realistic technique of writing employed by Flaubert in all of them and, in a less evident form, his view of life in the modern world. This was not so obvious to earlier critics, and one who could not accept *Madame Bovary* sometimes felt more kindly toward *La Tentation*.

The critical reception accorded Flaubert's works is here presented under three classifications: the articles occasioned by *Madame Bovary*; the critical attitude toward *Salammbô*, *La Tentation*, and *Trois Contes* as a group; and finally, the attention given to *L'Education* and *Bouvard et Pécuchet*. These two last works have come into major prominence only recently and because of the similarity mentioned above they will be treated together. This division rests mostly, though not completely, upon the similarities of treatment for each of these groups of novels.

The early acceptance or rejection of Flaubert's works depended most heavily upon moralistic concern and realistic or romantic partisan feelings. Later American critics became more aware of his interest in form, construction, and techniques. More recently, evaluations of his works by symbolistically inclined critics have appeared along with those of the sociologists and the new critics. For an analysis of Flaubert's role in American literary thought, critical trends must be reviewed and placed in proper perspective. In this way, the richness or the aridity of Flaubert's contribution to American novelistic art and the reaction engendered here by this contribution can be determined and appreciated.

II

THE SIGNIFICANCE OF FLAUBERT
FOR AMERICAN READERS

The United States was much slower in preparing for and accepting realism in the novel than was France. When *Madame Bovary* was published as a completely realistic treatment of a realistic subject there was, to be sure, a violent reaction against it in Paris. Its acceptance was not easy. But a full-blown school of realistic writers soon appeared who forged ahead and firmly established this type of novel.[1] The growth of this school was partly due to the fact that writers of the stature and genius of Flaubert, Zola, Daudet, the Goncourt brothers, and others practiced realism in their works with great artistry and force. Realism would perhaps not have gained strength if these early realistic novels had not been of the highest artistic caliber.

In America in the mid-nineteenth century there was no such school of established writers who practiced completely realistic techniques while maintaining a reputation for artistic excellence. Thus, when Flaubert first came to the attention of American critics, several conditions had to be satisfied. First, and most important, he had to present a clearly developed set of literary ideals which were solidly demonstrated by his work. In Flaubert's case, the canon he represented was at odds with currently accepted literary practices. He was a realist, and realism in 1860 was not in favor. Nevertheless, as his works appeared in the United States and drew attention, American critics could discern in them the application of the literary techniques which he favored and which were calling forth wider discussion than had previously been the case.

The growing critical notice Flaubert's works received here was also

[1] F. Steegmuller, *Flaubert and Madame Bovary* (New York, The Viking Press, 1950), p. 345.

bolstered by the widespread diffusion of his works in America. New literary ideals as represented by a single author often draw critical comment. But this recognition is sometimes of short duration unless the author's work catches the public imagination. Throughout the years Flaubert's novels have been the center of critical discussion because of the large numbers of readers they attracted in the United States.

Moreover, the climate of opinion in the latter half of the nineteenth century favored a centering of attention upon Flaubert's works. The appeal of new literary techniques and popular approval are not of long duration if the general climate of opinion is totally adverse to what an author represents. The acceptance of ideas and their diffusion require conditions which, if they are not completely favorable, at least offer some ground in which the ideas may take root and grow. Flaubert's works have enjoyed a great deal of popularity here, in some cases fleeting, in others enduring. This would indicate that Flaubert as an author had something new and permanent to give to literature and that he found a receptive condition in America for his ideals.

A. LITERARY IDEALS AND WORKS

Flaubert was born in 1821 in the early romantic period. This environment strongly colored his youthful inclinations and early literary endeavors.[2] It was during his early youth that he developed his inclination to solitude and his dislike of banality and platitude. These qualities are often pointed out in his work as a manifestation of pessimism. In reality they were the outgrowth of early romantic attitudes which developed into a distrust of and regret at the leveling tendencies of modern life.[3]

Early in life Flaubert turned to literature as a means of expressing his resentment at the preoccupation of society with unimportant ideas and ideals. His early works were highly romantic in style, but con-

---

[2] R. Descharmes, *Flaubert, sa vie, son caractère et ses idées avant 1857* (Paris, Librairie des Amateurs, A. Ferroud, 1909).

[3] R. Dumesnil, *Gustave Flaubert* (Paris, Desclée de Brouwer et Cie, 1932), p. 75.

tained the germ of several later works.[4] His desire to write was finally satisfied when, in 1843, after a serious illness, he moved to La Croisset outside Rouen, and devoted his entire attention to writing.

In 1849 he finished his first book seriously intended for publication. Its title was *La Tentation de Saint Antoine*. The theme of this work had fascinated Flaubert for many years and he was greatly pleased at having put it in book form. In great excitement and anticipation Flaubert called together his two dearest friends and critics, Marcel DuCamp and Louis Bouilhet. For a day and a night, until the end was reached, he read the book to them. During the long reading neither had made a comment. Then, with forbearance and humility, Flaubert listened to their opinion that he should cast the product of his long labor into the fire.[5] They severely criticized his lyricism. They told him to rid himself of his romantic tendencies and to treat a subject which would lend itself to a natural tone and a familiar style, to eliminate digressions from his work and to stick to the development of one concept. Flaubert followed his friends' instructions only to the extent of casting his manuscript into a drawer.

In spite of the lyrical style criticized by his two friends, Flaubert was temperamentally ready in 1850 to write his masterpiece, *Madame Bovary*. His dislike of the bourgeoisie and its tendency toward the acceptance of ready-made opinions and platitudes was evident in his early letters and in the *"Garçon"*,[6] an invention of his childhood. His pessimistic acceptance of life and its sadness is evident in his attitude toward his own illness. This acceptance, often almost serene, led him to seek a life apart at Croisset, after his convalescence, where he could contemplate life at a distance and create as he wished. He knew that this retreat was necessary for him. In a letter of 1846 he wrote:

J'ai fait nettement pour mon usage deux parts dans le monde et dans moi, d'un côté l'élément externe, que je désire varié, multicolore, harmonique, immense, mais dont je n'accepte rien que le spectacle d'en jouir; de l'autre,

---

[4]   A. Coleman, *Flaubert's Literary Development in the Light of His Mémoires d'un fou, Novembre, and Education sentimentale* (Baltimore, The Johns Hopkins University Press, 1941).

[5]   F. Steegmuller, *op. cit.*, p. 136.

[6]   The *"Garçon"* is a mythical character invented by Flaubert and his childhood friends to typify all the detestable traits of the bourgeoisie and its love of platitude.

l'élément interne, que je concentre afin de le rendre plus dense, et dans lequel je laisse pénétrer, à pleines effleuves, les plus purs rayons de l'esprit par la fenêtre ouverte de l'intelligence.[7]

Instead of active participation in life Flaubert chose observation from a reserved distance so that he could analyze himself and the world.

Art provided the mental retreat for Flaubert from the necessity of participating actively in the colorful, exciting, but also distressing and disturbing functions of life. Instead of turning to religion, philosophy, or science, he turned to art and there set his vocation and determined his future existence. In a letter of 1835, he affirmed this ideal in the following words: "Occupons-nous toujours de l'Art qui, plus grand que les peuples, les couronnes, et le rois, est toujours là suspendu dans l'enthousiasme, avec son diadème de Dieu." [8] Art represented the universal and the stable for him. He found it glorious, meriting his complete attention.

Flaubert had a high respect for art as an ideal standing alone. Coupled with this respect was his desire to stand apart from active participation in life and his fatalistic acceptance of the blows dealt him by fortune. These factors contributed greatly to his well-defined idea of impersonality in art. In 1836 he wrote, "L'Art est un principe complet en lui-même, et qui n'a pas plus besoin d'appui qu'une étoile." [9] He did not like explanatory passages or prefaces whereby the author introduced himself and his thoughts directly before the reader's eye. For this reason he criticized Balzac's *Comédie Humaine* which he found basically objective but filled with reflections of a political, philosophical, and sociological nature.[10] He felt that a writer who takes his own personality as the subject of a poem or novel and makes his own adventures their subject matter, or even one who explicitly gives a subjective opinion upon that which he is describing can never express complete general truth, but only part of the truth. The conclusion to be drawn should be implicit in the work. The author has failed if he has to explain. Flaubert expressed this thought strongly by writing that "L'ineptie consiste à vouloir conclure. . . . Oui, la bêtise consiste à

[7] Flaubert, Gustave, *Correspondance* (Paris, Charpentier, 1891-1894), I, p. 139.
[8] *Ibid.*, I, p. 13.
[9] *Ibid.*, I, p. 131.
[10] R. Dumesnil, *op. cit.*, p. 42.

vouloir conclure. Nous sommes un fil et nous voulons savoir la trame."[11] Above all, he felt that the author should never attempt to contrive conclusions. The writer's task is to represent, not to try to justify events. These must flow naturally and form their own justification. The fact of existence is the justification for existence. "A quoi bon les mauvaises herbes, disent les brave gens? Pourquoi poussent-elles? Mais pour elles-mêmes, par Dieu! Pourquoi poussez-vous, vous?",[12] Flaubert asked of the authors who required a logical sequence of events and a straightforward conclusion. Nevertheless, his impersonality did not signify an inhuman detachment from every emotion, painful or pleasant. It meant simply a rejection of the personal and subjective only in so far as these qualities distort or vitiate art. If an author expresses his own opinions he will limit thereby the operations of his characters, he will hamper them with irrelevant intrusions and destroy the general truth by reducing it to a personal prejudice. Flaubert did not rule out moral judgment, but he wanted it to be implicit in the facts rather than expressed in the text.

Philip Spencer wrote that:

In Flaubert they [the readers] have someone alive to every moment of his age; its tensions are focussed onto his anguished sensibility and his personal disequilibrium incarnates and condenses the general disequilibrium about him. At the same time he masters his sensibility and interprets it as an artist; and he formulates his own canons and obeys them with such unswerving rectitude that he becomes a symbolic figure, the patriarch of fiction, the prototype of the stylist.[13]

The enormous respect that Flaubert held for art as an innate principle led him inevitably to regard form as a basic and essential component of any work of art. For him sense and form were inextricably intertwined; one was not possible without the other. And the more perfect the form, the more perfect and true was the sense. He had formulated this concept before beginning his work on *Bovary* and expressed it in a letter in the following words:

Tant qu'on ne m'aura pas, une phrase donnée, séparé la forme du fond, je soutiendrai que ce sont là des mots vides de sens ... Du même que tu

---

[11] *Correspondance*, I, p. 338.
[12] *Ibid.*, I, p. 141.
[13] *Flaubert* (London, Faber and Faber Ltd., 1952), p. 147.

ne peux extraire d'un corps physique les qualités qui le constituent, c'est
à dire couleur, étendue, solidité, sans le réduire à une abstraction creuse,
sans le détruire, en un mot, de même tu n'ôteras pas la forme de l'idée,
car l'idée n'existe qu'en vertu de sa forme. Supposer une idée qui n'ait
pas de forme, c'est impossible, de même qu'une forme qui n'exprime pas
une idée.[14]

This concept led Flaubert to a long and difficult effort toward perfection of style which he considered requisite to perfect expression of
ideas. His constant concern with sound, rhythm, fitness, and quality
of his composition in *Madame Bovary* is a legend. His concern revo-
lutionized the art of the novel.

Preparation for *Madame Bovary* was nearly complete by 1850. He
had already acquired the predisposition to the objective and scientific
observation of facts, and the recording of those facts in a reserved and
withdrawn manner. His temperament was one of resigned pessimism
tinged with a repugnance for the so-called bourgeois aspects of his
environment. He had an extreme regard for art and form. All he
lacked was a subject.

The dependence of Flaubert on local color and real facts drawn
from life and experience in Normandy for the creation of *Madame
Bovary* is a well-established fact.[15] All of his descriptions are drawn
from real life and the types for all of his characters may be observed to
this day in the cities and towns of that region. It has also been definitely confirmed that the tale upon which the novel is based was an actual
event which happened in the Delamare family who were among the
friends of the Flauberts.[16] The background of the story was completely
familiar to him. He knew firsthand all the aspects of rural Norman
medical practice. The countrified dullness of Delamare and his wife's
bourgeois sacrifice to romanticism were ideally suited to his talents.
Flaubert did protest against the vulgarity of the subject, but Bouilhet
insisted that it was one best suited to his ideas and tendencies. He
needed to write in a strictly realistic manner devoid of all the romantic
bombast and lyricism of his *Saint Antoine*. Here was a subject which

[14]   *Correspondance*, I, p. 157.
[15]   J. Canu, "La Couleur Normande chez *Madame Bovary*", *PMLA*, XLVIII
(1933), p. 167.
[16]   F. Steegmuller, *op. cit.*, p. 218.

would lend itself to such treatment. After some thought and temporizing, Flaubert decided to utilize the material and chose a title, *Madame Bovary*, for his novel.

Madame Bovary represented a crucial stage in the development of Flaubert's technique. He had analyzed in detail his romantic view of the world and its effect on personal relations. Writing this novel helped drain away some of the contempt and bitterness which he felt toward the bourgeoisie. This is evident in Homais, the character in the novel who turns out to be not a caricature of bourgeois stupidity but a living being with a forceful personality. Though Flaubert's early romantic spirit was repressed in the writing of this book, he retained some of its characteristics: love of fine language, use of irony, fatalism in the chain of intrinsically harmless events and situations linked together to lead to Emma's downfall, distrust of life, and his view of a hostile world and disdain for its standards of success.

In 1856 *Madame Bovary* appeared in serialized form in France and created a sensation. The *"succès de scandale"* which this version created made possible the publication in book form the next year. Flaubert's tale of the dreary aspects of provincial life, the degeneration of Emma Bovary because of her addiction to romantic dreams, and her weak-willed subservience to her passions created a furore among the critics and the public unused to such unrelievedly realistic presentation. Several scenes were severely criticized, notably the one where Emma received the last rites of the church. The forthright description of the dying spasms of the heroine was shocking to the reader who was used to romantic depictions of repentance and peaceful demise. There was a feeling that Flaubert had attacked the religious institutions with his ironic descriptions and that he had criticized the final comfort which the church offered.

The critics were much less favorable in their opinions than was the general public. The large sale of the work showed the public's approval. But the critics called the book crude, heartless, false and unrealistic, a huge heap of dung, a morbid exaltation of the senses and imagination, a pamphlet against humanity. Baudelaire was one of the few sympathetic critics, as was Sainte-Beuve. They expressed appreciation for the fresh approach to novel writing and the effective use of realistic details and techniques. Barbey d'Aurevilley best sensed what

Flaubert had accomplished and offered warm praise.[17] But not all of the important literary figures were able to understand what *Madame Bovary* represented in the development of novelistic techniques. Even Duranty, the advocate of realism, castigated Flaubert in his journal, *Le Réalisme*, for having created a book which was "calculated, overworked, all right-angled, arid and dry".[18]

The realism of *Madame Bovary* was too novel to be immediately acceptable to the French critics. They had become accustomed to the realism of Scarron, Furetière, Lesage, and Marivaux where realistic details were mixed with gaiety and satire. Frequent changes in tone and content amused the reader. The realism of Balzac and Stendhal had been interspersed with flights of romanticism and fancy. Thus, these earlier works were more palatable. Flaubert's realism was wholly realistic in conception and execution. It was a bitter draught to those unaccustomed to the taste.[19]

This initial distaste gradually changed in France to appreciation, especially after publication of some of Flaubert's later works. A realization of the importance of his methods and theories in their application to novel writing soon manifested itself. Other French novelists became partisans of Flaubertian realism and quietly adopted his techniques. French writers still do so. René Descharmes wrote of Flaubert that "Il est, avec Balzac, le véritable créateur du roman moderne. Maupassant, Zola, et Daudet sont bien de sa descendance directe; mais les écrivains qui se croient fort éloignés d'appartenir au naturalisme et affectent de battre en brèche ses principes surannées, trahissent encore souvent, par leur style ou par leur méthode de composition l'influence qu'ils ont reçue du premier de ses représentants." [20]

The publication of *Madame Bovary* made Flaubert famous. It also established the canons of his craft. In it one can see in concrete form all the esthetic ideals created by the author and an entirely original literary form created by their application. But this fame was bitter to Flaubert. He was disappointed because of the lawsuit which he had to fight in order to have his book accepted as morally fit for the con-

---

[17]   See Philip Spencer, *op. cit.*, p. 130.
[18]   *Ibid.*, p. 138.
[19]   E. Faguet, *Gustave Flaubert* (Boston, Houghton Mifflin and Co., 1914), p. 89.
[20]   R. Descharmes, *op. cit.*, p. 1.

sumption of the French reading public. Nor did Flaubert earn much money from it, since he had made an arrangement with his publisher which was hardly favorable to himself. For all of these reasons and because of his personal inclinations, he decided to change his literary directions and write a novel with an entirely different background. Instead of describing a contemporary period, he proposed to return to the past. The setting would be Carthage, and the background derived from a civilization which was almost unknown even to archeologists. This, of course, meant an enormous amount of research in order to establish the foundation upon which Flaubert would create his characters and the events of the story. The idea of huge amounts of research was not counter to his inclinations and he happily set to work on *Salammbô*.

Salammbô was published in 1863. Here again Flaubert was faced with unfriendly criticism and scorching denunciations. The book was criticized for inaccuracies of fact and background, for immoral tendencies, and for paganistic teachings. But the public found it to its taste and the sale of *Salammbô* was large from the very beginning. Along with the increase in his reading public, Flaubert's reputation was growing, both in France and outside its boundaries. He was encouraged by this appreciation, though his attitude was never that of an author eager for an adulating public. He wrote to please himself and was happy when he found readers who understood and liked his work.

After the publication of *Salammbô*, Flaubert turned his mind to two projects which had been important to him for many years. One was the development of the novel, *L'Education sentimentale*, derived from his earlier effort *Novembre*; the other was the *Tentation de Saint Antoine* which he had never discarded as he had been advised to do. Most of his work during this period from 1863 to 1869 went into *L'Education sentimentale*, published in 1869. It was not a new experience for Flaubert to have his works severely criticized on their publication, but both the critical and the public dislike of this work was particularly strong. It was not until the mid-twentieth century that the book was to claim its place beside *Madame Bovary* as a great masterpiece. Today there are those who rank it highest among Flaubert's works.

Flaubert became intensely involved in this book. Though he based the central plot upon an event in his own life, the story was not auto-biographical. Again, Flaubert was not describing the particular but showing the general. The main story is closely woven into a broad pattern of contemporary life. Essentially the subject of *L'Education sentimentale* is man and his reactions to and relations with currents of thought and attitudes during the years 1840 to 1851, the decline and fall of Louis Philippe, the establishment of the Second Republic, and finally, the regime of Louis Napoleon. It gives a diagnosis of social and political ills of the time. But it was a poor moment to publish a book of this nature. Both the critics and the public let it alone. It was regarded as merely a dull example of photographic presentation. Because they were so close to the events described, readers were unable to see the work in its proper perspective. They could not appreciate, without the advantage of a distant perspective, the vast amount of research which was required to create a true image of life. Instead, the work was thought to be a misanthropic satire and an unnatural view of life. Nevertheless, in his attempts to portray a period of history employing a background made up of physical details and intellectual aspects which were all integral to the plot, Flaubert deeply influenced the history of the realistic novel.

In 1874, five years after the publication of *L'Education*, Flaubert published *La Tentation de Saint Antoine*. As already indicated, the subject of this work was one which had haunted his mind for many years. The 1849 version contained a philosophic message which was ill-defined. Most of the emphasis was placed upon the description, in vivid color and detail, of the temptation of the hermit. His later version represented the intellectualization of this same temptation. It gave to the episode a more generalized significance which applied to all mankind rather than solely to the ascetic recluse. Again Flaubert devoted an enormous amount of time and energy to research. When he had finished he had acquired a record of nearly every philosophic and religious movement in history. He created *La Tentation de Saint Antoine* as a representative picture of humanity's struggle to achieve the truth rather than a personal vision of one man's struggle against the excesses of the flesh and the troubles of the spirit. His Saint Anthony was not tempted primarily by bodily desires but was consumed by a thirst to know Truth. His excesses had been translated from the sphere of emotion and sense to that of idea; he discussed and argued, but never achieved his purpose because absolute truth is unknowable to man. In this final version sin, logic, science, and the pig had disappeared. Instead, what each of them represented had been recapitulated in the beginning of the book. All of the temptations had been intellectualized and Saint Anthony's desire for complete and innate knowledge was expressed in his final outburst, "O bonheur! bonheur! J'ai vu naître la vie, j'ai vu le mouvement commencer. J'ai envie de voler, de nager ... me blottir sous toutes les formes, pénétrer chaque atome, descendre jusqu'au fond de la matière, être la matière." The book is difficult to read because the erudition it contains is combined with flights of spirit so faithfully rendered that the total effect is wearisome. But in spite of the absolute care spent in technique, and in spite of the mass of detail, the style, form, and content blend perfectly into an inspiring and poetic rendition of one man's search for an ultimate meaning in life.

The reception accorded *La Tentation* by the critics differed little from that given his previous works. Though discouraged, Flaubert was not disillusioned. The three years following its publication were to see the appearance of the stories which make up the *Trois Contes*.

There were many friends in the literary world who understood what Flaubert was trying to do and who let him know it. One of these was Georges Sand. She valued Flaubert as a writer even though she did not approve of his artistic impersonality and impartiality. She could not see why he should refrain from moralizing. She suggested that he write something to prove to the public that he was sensitive and had a love for humanity. The result was *Un Cœur simple* (1876). Unfortunately, some of the French critics were predisposed to the idea of Flaubert in the role of misanthropist, the critic of humanity instead of its champion. The picture he had drawn was too real and fresh, in spite of the love and warmth shining through the description of the faithful and simple servant.

Flaubert defended himself against this type of easy evaluation. Of *Un Cœur simple* he wrote: "Cela est nullement ironique, comme vous le supposez, mais, au contraire, très sérieux et très triste. Je veux appitoyer, faire pleurer les âmes sensibles, en étant une moi-même." [21]

---

[21]   See A. Thibaudet, *Gustave Flaubert* (Paris, Librairie Plon, 1922), p. 158.

Flaubert at this time knew the meaning of sacrifice and resignation, having impoverished himself for his niece and her husband and then having suffered their rebuffs because he refused to beg for charity so that they could continue their extravagant way of life. Furthermore, he had modelled the old servant in his tale on the servant of his childhood (Julie) whom he loved and respected. In this tale he dispensed with all irony and mockery, and gave way to sad pity. The life of the servant is depicted with great simplicity. Flaubert described it as a series of events not pressing forward to a hopeless future, but instead depicting a hopeful and simple present. The pattern of events shows that an uncritical, humble life of sacrifice possesses meaning and beauty.

La Légende de Saint Julien L'Hospitalier appeared in 1876 just before the publication of *Un Cœur simple*. While writing the latter, Flaubert was planning another short tale on a biblical theme. This story, *Hérodias*, appeared in 1877, and the same year Charpentier published the three tales together under the title *Trois Contes*. All three of these tales were composed with the same careful attention to detail and perfection of form as were the longer novels. They won Flaubert many ardent friends and grateful readers. For once critical acclaim was almost unanimous in favor of these three tales.

Flaubert's last major work, *Bouvard et Pécuchet*, was left unfinished because of his death in 1880. Ezra Pound has called this book the forerunner of a new genre in the style of Swift, Rabelais, and Cervantes. At the end of his life Flaubert thus attempted to write his ultimate message in what he considered the ultimate literary form, that is, a novel about life in which nothing happens. None of his contemporaries understood the book and all of them rejected it. It is only within the last thirty years that critics have begun to take it seriously, though there are still many who consider the book unreadable. For those who like it, it is a superbly funny book which treats of a basic weakness of humanity.

In nineteenth century France it was a common opinion among artistic people that bourgeois democracy brought about the death of the mind, beauty, literature, and greatness. *Bouvard et Pécuchet* was a protest against these destructive aspects of democracy. In it we see satirized bourgeois stupidity, moral weakness, political falseness and artistic makeshift. This book depicts the widespread affliction of modern life. It attacked the tendency of the modern world to believe that knowledge is obtained with no mental or physical effort. Flaubert made a farce of human pretensions to encyclopedic knowledge. Today, more than at any other previous period, man is capable of understanding and appreciating the message contained in this work. However, the writers who admired and emulated Flaubert during his lifetime were not unduly impressed by this posthumous book.

After the publication of *Madame Bovary*, Flaubert became the central figure of a literary group which was trying to revolutionize French letters. The publication of his later works established him even more firmly in this position. He was quickly accepted by the members of the group composed of Zola, the Goncourts, Daudet, and others who looked to him as their chief, for in *Madame Bovary* he had created the model for the new techniques which were called "naturalistic". Although the sensation created by the works of Zola soon overshadowed the novels of Flaubert in the public eye, this sensation did not diminish the importance given by his fellow writers to his works because of their intrinsic greatness. Critics still refer to Flaubert as the leader of the naturalists. W. C. Frierson wrote concerning *Madame Bovary*:

> The book established the type of the "naturalistic" or "experimental" novel, and is the basis of the principles according to which much of the fiction of the Concourts, Zola, Maupassant, Turgenief, George Moore, Henry James, and Arnold Bennett was written. Those of the contemporary novelists who seek in fiction to give a conscious expression of reality consider the reading of the work a necessary act of apprenticeship.[22]

This appellation "naturalistic" is unfortunate. For though Flaubert worked in much the same framework as did Zola, there are such fundamental differences between the books and the objectives of Zola and those of Flaubert that the two writers should not be classed in the same category.

The methods of Zola and Flaubert differed radically. Zola thought he was much more the true scientist in his technique than did Flaubert. The latter had more concern for art than for science, and he was not unwilling to set aside the scientific principles of naturalism in order

---

[22]   W. C. Frierson, "The Naturalistic Techniques of Flaubert", *The French Quarterly*, VII (1925), p. 178.

to achieve greater purity of art. Zola thought that in literature he had found a humanitarian weapon to combat human and social ills as he saw them. He was a reformer, which Flaubert never pretended to be. Flaubert employed naturalistic techniques only in so far as he found them an effective means of creating the art forms he wished to achieve. Though he clarified for his reader his vision of man in a modern environment and the problems posed by the setting, his purpose was never sociological. There was no need of preaching or moralizing because any conclusions to be drawn were implicit in the material.

In an attempt to explain just what elements made up his method, Flaubert wrote the following in a letter to Louise Colet:

Il y a en moi, littérairement parlant, deux bonshommes distincts; un qui est épris de gueulades, de lyrisme, de grands vols d'aigles, de toutes les sonorités de la phrase et des sommets de l'idée, un autre qui fouille et creuse le vrai tant qu'il peut, qui aime à accuser le petit fait aussi puissamment que le grand, qui voudrait vous faire sentir presque matériellement les choses qu'il a reproduites; celui-là aime à rire et se plaît dans les animalités de l'homme. L'*Education sentimentale* (de 1848) a été, à mon insu, un effort de fusion entre ces deux tendences de mon esprit (il eut été plus facile de faire de l'humain dans un livre et du lyrisme dans un autre).[23]

Flaubert taught that a scientific observation of exterior details was necessary. He insisted that all of the details be truthful and faithful copies of life. The unusual and striking detail was rejected in favor of the ordinary and the true. He felt that the commonplace held more verity than the spectacular. For this reason his effects were created by an accumulation of facts rather than by a striking instance, and his most successful subjects were the temporal ones. All the romantic characteristics of literature which interfered with the unity of his story were cast aside. He never intruded into his plot by moralizing or casting judgements. The structure of the novels was firmly knit and all of the action led directly to the end, revealing in the entire structure the whole meaning of the work. In order to achieve this, there was an essential need for art.

Flaubert's great attention to art showed up the literature of the Second Empire as unreal and inartistic. Emile Faguet pointed out how

[23]   See R. Dumesnil, *op. cit.*, p. 345.

Flaubert's innovations contributed to the decline of Champfleury, Achard, Feuillet, Dumas *fils*, and others.[24] Flaubert proved that by rigidly applying the criteria which he had established, one could achieve a true representation of life itself in its complexities and in its precise details. He described people and things simultaneously and without confusion so that in his descriptions the surroundings and characters, all maintaining their proper place, appear unified before the reader. His realistic novel presents a picture of average humanity where the noble and the elevated are the exception.

Before Flaubert the novel had almost exclusively treated plot, development of characters, the suitability of sentiment and the dramatic action and its progression. He introduced the concept of marriage of content with form. He created style by attempting to make his expression conform absolutely to the level of sensation and thought. He believed that style must obey physiological laws; if a sentence is good, its pulsations will agree with the heart, its respiration will harmonize with that of the reader; if it is bad, it will interfere with the cardiac rhythm and oppress the lungs.

Though much of the moral criticism that Flaubert received was due to his scientific and esthetic approach to literature, he felt that he must base his style upon a scientific approach to writing. He wrote that "Les faits agissent sur nous et nous les causons. . . . Pourquoi ne pas avoir trouvé (à vos héros) une fin en rapport naturel avec leur antécédents? Cela est de la fantaisie et donne à une œuvre sérieusement commencée des apparences légères. Le roman, selon moi, doit être scientifique, c'est à dire, rester dans les généralités probables." [25] Flaubert's scientific method, the classification and examination of phenomena, was not concerned with the exceptional. His search was for the characteristic of the individual or the situation he was describing. Having found this permanent characteristic, he employed it as an immutable law to create a common effect applicable to general circumstances. He felt that the author should not concern himself with the accidental, particular details, but should seek deeply for the definitive aspect, not merely representing one single thing but things in their generality.

Here is where the artist replaced the scientist in making the choice

---

[24]   *Flaubert*, p. 129.
[25]   See R. Dumesnil, *op. cit.*, p. 324.

and in eliminating the non-essential. Flaubert used a deterministic method in his craft, but it was employed in an artistic way. As an artist, Flaubert determined *a priori* his general concept and consciously endowed it with the proper gestures, language, and whatever was necessary to give the concept reality. He started with the individual fact and worked toward the universal. His imagination was at work, but not in a subjective fashion. His scientific attitudes established the objectivity which Flaubert desired. He never allowed *a priori* ideas to express anything personal in his works. What he expressed was controlled by what he saw. He attempted to discover all aspects of all things, not only the aspects which satisfied his personal tastes and desires. His attention to style and the artistic qualities of his works made impossible the mechanical representation which this technique might engender. For Flaubert objects had a moral and a physical side, an interior and an exterior world. But one had to observe them with an artistic vision. To writers he said: "Regardez les choses assez long-temps et avec assez d'attention pour découvrir un aspect qui n'ait été vu ni dit par personne." [26]

Art for Flaubert was the one essential quality in any work. He believed that only in art could meaning and values be established. His realism was tempered by esthetic considerations which had never before been so definitely stated and so consistently employed. He spent years composing his books in a manner which would insure their artistic perfection. All his efforts were directed toward the objective of creating a true picture of life with its exterior form and interior meaning fused into a vibrant, meaningful depiction of reality in its generality.

The publication of Flaubert's books in France and the growing importance that he achieved as an innovator in literary techniques occurred at the same time that important developments were taking place on the American literary scene. Flaubert's reputation spread beyond the boundaries of France to the United States. His ideas were discussed here in the regularly scheduled articles on French literature which appeared in the leading magazines. He and his works quickly created interest because of the impending battle which was soon to break out between the romantics and the realists in America. Once

[26]   *Ibid.*, p. 418.

established, the interest shown in the works of Flaubert by American critics and readers has endured up to the present. The great number of editions of his works which have appeared in the United States in translation has made Flaubert one of the foreign writers best known to the American public.[27]

B. DIFFUSION OF FLAUBERT'S WORKS IN AMERICA

The first English translation of *Madame Bovary* did not appear in America until 1881, twenty-four years after its publication in France.[28] But the American reader was aware of Flaubert as a major force in contemporary literature. His name was known here long before the publication of the first English version of his first novel. Articles in the *Atlantic Monthly, Lippincott's Magazine, Nation*, and others with good circulation made Flaubert the topic of much discussion.

The increasing mention of Flaubert in magazines was due to the fact that he represented so clearly to the critics the new techniques of realism in French literature. And realism had become a *cause célèbre* among the literary critics in America during the latter half of the nineteenth century. Flaubert was cited as the initiator of the movement in France and used as an example of the results of such a treatment in literature.

Another factor which made his novels a subject of interest for the American critic and reader was the scandal caused in France by the publication of *Madame Bovary* and its subsequent court trial. The first notices about Flaubert or his work which appeared in the United States dealt at length with his morality. A strong feeling existed that he treated subjects not spoken of in refined society. He represented a cold, materialistic approach to literature which left little or nothing to the imagination. His characters were, according to American critics, sunk in vice and degradation.[29]

---

[27] See Appendix B for list of English translations of Flaubert's works which have appeared in America.

[28] *Madame Bovary*, trans. John Stirling, pseud. (Philadelphia, T. B. Peterson and Bros., 1881).

[29] See Appendix A, 4, 6, 9, 10, 11, 12, 14, 15, 16.

Some laudatory articles did appear to combat the general impression of these derogatory reviews.[30] They claimed that *Madame Bovary* was in reality a very moral book since it did not reward vice nor corruption as was generally thought. In addition, they praised Flaubert's attempts to revolutionize novel writing and to open up new, wider avenues to the young writer who was dissatisfied with the limitations imposed by the romantic school.

The T. B. Peterson and Brothers cheap edition of *Madame Bovary* designed for wide distribution was followed shortly by two other like editions put out by Rand McNally and by Munroe. The cheap edition was intended for the ordinary reader and the distribution was wide. Many features of these cheap editions were regrettable. Mott[31] pointed out how they encouraged literary piracy and price cutting tricks. Much that came out in these editions was not good literature and was badly bound. On the other hand, these houses did publish a great deal of fine literature and made it available to the great popular audience who could not afford the expensive editions. Mott found that this was the case with *Madame Bovary*. In the 1880's best sellers developed among what were considered "forbidden" French novels. "Then Zola's *Nana* and Flaubert's *Madame Bovary,* both studies of courtesan's lives were brought into the cheap 'libraries'. Of course *Madame Bovary* had been published many years before in France, but it received its chief impetus in America when Peterson, Munroe, and Rand McNally, and other publishers of cheap novels took it up. Including recent sales in the twenty-five cent editions, it is probable that each of these novels has reached the million mark in America." [32]

It is impossible today to discover how many copies of *Madame Bovary* were sold in the eighties and nineties. One may safely assume that they were numerous. Enthusiasm for certain books spread widely throughout the country "with all the exaggerations and delirium of eulogy that followed upon such epidemics".[33] *Madame Bovary* seems to have benefited from such an enthusiasm. At least seven editions of the novel were published from 1881 to 1900. *Salammbô*, when it

[30] *Ibid.,* 3, 13, 17, 18.
[31] *Golden Multitudes,* p. 240.
[32] *Ibid.,* p. 248.
[33] *Ibid.,* p. 183.

was published in translation in 1885, benefited from the popularity of the earlier work and had at least five editions during the same period. After the turn of the century Flaubert was firmly established as a good-selling novelist in America. The book-buying public was purchasing his novels for current reading and made the publication of the cheaper editions profitable ventures for the publishing houses. More expensive editions and some luxury editions were also published for those who wished to include his works in their libraries. In 1896 an expensive edition of *Madame Bovary* for subscribers only was published (Philadelphia, G. Barrie and Son). Another appeared in 1905 (Connoisseur edition, New York, Société des Beaux Arts), and two in 1950 (New York, Limited Editions Club and Heritage Press). *Salammbô* came out in a luxury edition in 1935 (National Home Library Foundation, Washinton, D.C.). In 1943 the New York Limited Editions Club published the *Temptation of Saint Anthony*. Also two expensive editions of the *Complete Works* appeared, one printed for subscribers only by the M. W. Dunne Company of New York in 1904, the other in ten volumes, published in 1935 by the Dingwell Rock Company of New York.

Since 1881 the total number of American editions of the various novels by Flaubert amounts to well over one hundred.[34] *Madame Bovary* from the beginning has proved to be the most popular seller among his novels. It has appeared in at least forty-four editions here. More than a dozen different translations into English have been made of this work. That done by Eleanor Marx-Aveling has been the longest-lived with frequent republication by various publishing houses since 1901. Superior translations of *Madame Bovary* are the more recent ones. They excel both in capturing the original flavor and spirit of the novel and in a rendition into English which reflects Flaubert's high regard for style and harmony. One is by Gerard Hopkins (New York, Oxford University Press, 1949) and the other by Francis Steegmuller (New York, Random House, 1957) who has also translated Flaubert's letters and written fine critical evaluations of his work. *Salammbô* follows *Madame Bovary* in the number of American

[34] See Appendix B for list of English translations of Flaubert's works published in America.

editions with twenty-three. The most satisfactory translation of this novel has been done by J. C. Chartres.[35] The most recent available editions of this translation appeared in 1956, published in New York by E. P. Dutton. Mention should be made of the fine translation done by Lafcadio Hearn of *La Tentation de Saint Antoine* [36] where he preserved in English the feeling and color of the original French work. A good translation of *L'Education sentimentale* has been made by Anthony Goldsmith (New York, E. P. Dutton, 1957) and of *Bouvard et Pécuchet* by Stonier and Earp (Norfolk, Connecticut, New Directions, 1954).

The first marked upswing in interest in Flaubert's works as manifested by increase in publication of his works occurred after 1900. From 1900 to 1920 twenty-three different editions of various novels by him were presented to the American public. Except during the years of the Second World War the rate of publication remained high. In the decade of the 1930's the high peak of interest was maintained here with sixteen editions of his works. In the 1950's the rate climbed again to seventeen different editions. *Salammbô* has not maintained the high rate of popularity which it enjoyed at first. *Madame Bovary* remains a favorite. *L'Education sentimentale* and *Bouvard et Pécuchet* are growing in popularity.[37]

The public enthusiasm for the works of Flaubert was aided by the interest shown in him by American critics. Their treatment of his literary value and aims heightened public interest and gave prestige to the popularity which Flaubert enjoyed. This began as early as 1881 with the publication of the translation of *Madame Bovary*. Maxime DuCamp's *Souvenirs littéraires* appeared at the same time in Paris. He described Flaubert's literary aims and principles and thus enabled the American critics to evaluate more accurately what the author of *Madame Bovary* was attempting to do and provided more material for critical notices.[38]

These notices were more favorable in tone, professing to find in

---

[35]   Chicago, Charles H. Sergel and Co., 1891.
[36]   New York, Alice Hariman Co., 1910.
[37]   See Appendix B for recent editions of these works.
[38]   See Appendix A, 22, 24, 25, 26, 27.

Flaubert traces of romanticism which softened his harsh realism. The greatest boon to the American critic was the first book written in English about Flaubert, J. C. Tarver's *Gustave Flaubert as Seen in his Works and Correspondence.*[39] The appearance of this book generated an interest on the part of the critics to discuss at great length Flaubert's literary technique and his life.[40]

The change from a popular to a scholarly emphasis in studies on Flaubert became evident in the second decade of the twentieth century. Madame Bovary especially has been used as a text in many courses in novel writing, world literature, and the study of the English or American novel. In very recent years the interest has begun to change from *Madame Bovary* to *L'Education sentimentale.* Critics and scholarly writers have disseminated a knowledge of Flaubert by using his works to illustrate the various aspects and techniques of the novelist's art. For many years he has been regarded by students of literature as one of the most important writers for the study of the novel.

Articles authored by Coleman and by Blossom of the Johns Hopkins University have appeared in *Modern Language Notes.*[41] Scholarly interest at this University was further manifested by an important publication concerning aspects of Flaubert's early influences and his style,[42] and also by the appearance of several scholarly books on the subject of Flaubert's sources and structure [43] and his literary development.[44] During this decade three doctoral dissertations on Flaubert were also written at the Johns Hopkins.[45]

The number of scholarly works and articles about Flaubert increased during the 1920's although the number of articles appearing in popular magazines was still large.[46] During the 1930's, however, the number of the articles in popular magazines decreased until the numerous articles about Flaubert were to be found almost exclusively in journals

[39]   New York, Appleton and Co., 1895.
[40]   See Appendix A, 64, 65, 66, 67, 68.
[41]   *Ibid.,* 103, 105, 107, 110, 151.
[42]   *Ibid.,* 115.
[43]   *Ibid.,* 112, 124.
[44]   *Ibid.,* 117.
[45]   See Appendix C for list of Ph. D. dissertations on the subject of Flaubert submitted to American universities.
[46]   See Appendix A, 128-165.

published at universities.[47] Since this time doctoral dissertations about Flaubert have appeared in increasing numbers.[48]

In short, twentieth-century critics, especially, have written of his works to demonstrate old or new methods of the craft of writing and articles have appeared with more and more frequency. In the forties, for example, interest in Flaubert's novels seemed to be centered on symbolism and symbolistic techniques. Engstrom, Tindall, Blackmur, and others called attention to his writings because of his pioneer work in this direction.[49] Lewisohn, Colum, Trilling, and Auerbach, among others, pointed out the modern view of society which was to be found in Flaubert's novels.[50] The liberal critics and students interested in this aspect of literature found much in his work to illustrate the lucid application of social consciousness in the novel. Finally, esthetic critics found in Flaubert's novels a useful elucidation of their viewpoint.[51] Flaubert had enunciated almost all the theories of esthetic criticism in his correspondence and had illustrated the theory in his works. Burke, Turnell, and Caroline Gordon, among a host of others, have found in his works the justification for the esthetic approach to literary criticism. He had consciously attempted to create his novels following principles of structure, semantics, and the fusion of exterior form with interior meaning. It was not difficult for the critic to point out the function of these principles in works in which they had so fully been put into practice.

Flaubert was not simply a "writer's writer" in America. The numerous publications of his novels, many of them in inexpensive popular editions, show that he has been a widely read author in this country. At the same time he has enjoyed the prestige of being studied by critics and scholars in the United States. They have helped to spread a knowledge about him and his work, and have also helped to increase the popularity of his novels. His reading public has included the critic, the student, and the general public. He has the distinction of being a best-selling author with the prestige of being sanctioned

---

[47]   *Ibid.*, 170 ff.
[48]   See Appendix C.
[49]   See Appendix A, 217, 219, 226, 249, 255, 267.
[50]   *Ibid.*, 158, 185, 191, 224, 250.
[51]   *Ibid.*, 214, 232, 267.

by respected authorities. The intensity of the interest manifested by American critics can be correlated, to some extent, with the literary and social atmosphere in which it was engendered. Some of the reasons for Flaubert's popular appeal can be found in the public demand for a literature embodying the qualities which his novels possessed. The literary climate which created the popular tastes had an effect on the critics too. Thus they studied Flaubert in an attempt to analyze the appeal which he might have for the contemporary reader. In doing so, they had to take into account the age in which they lived.

C. CLIMATE OF RECEPTION

The study of Flaubert's critical reception in America is inextricably woven into the developments which led to one of the greatest literary upheavals in American history. American critics became aware of his work early in the latter half of the nineteenth century and have continued their interest in it up to the present time. The years included in this period are represented also by the great struggle of romanticism versus realism and the development of the esthetic school of American criticism. Any meaningful interpretation which may be given to the American attitudes toward Flaubert must take into account the development of these literary trends and the effect which they had upon literary taste and opinions during the nearly one hundred years under consideration.

The social and intellectual climate that gave rise to the new ideals and points of view which entered into American criticism inevitably colored the evaluations of Flaubert which appeared during the period. He represented, sometimes too strongly for those American critics who were opposed to the new currents of realism, the ideals which gave birth to the literary battle here, especially in the last half of the nineteenth century. He helped to establish some of those ideals. At the least, he provided a good subject of controversy for the critics, both advocates and adversaries of the nineteenth century school of realism in the novel.

There were many indications of unrest between the romantic and the realist schools before 1860. The main struggle was most apparent after that date and came to a head in what Grant Knight calls the "critical years", 1890 to 1900.[52] Knight says that this struggle represented our first literary warfare on a major scale and that no such engagement before or since equalled it in seriousness or length.

In the first half of the nineteenth century it was romanticism that molded American critical tradition. This movement arrived late and full blown in America and was accepted without a struggle. Parrington points out how the early economic and geographic expansion and the intellectual and moral changes that accompanied the movement helped in the assimilation of the romantic cause here.[53] The tenets of romanticism were supported by Brockden Brown, Lowell, Whittier, Melville, Cooper, and others who were inspired to create the American counterpart of works like those of Scott and Wordsworth. In their attempt they created the first true American novels and poetry by turning their attention to local scenes and backgrounds. Cooper, Melville, and Hawthorne were strongly influenced by romanticism but were truly American in inspiration.

The emergence of an American literature gave impetus to a growing feeling of nationalism which manifested itself in our literary criticism. In 1837, Emerson in his Phi Beta Kappa address, "The American Scholar", hailed America's growing intellectual maturity and increasing independence from foreign influence in literature. It became an axiom among nationalistically inclined writers and critics that good American literature must be animated by an American spirit. The desire for a literature which was purely their own led American writers and critics to a closer examination of the literary trends and ideals which were influencing the direction taken by our writers. A suspicious approach to foreign imports and influences was adopted. At the same time, the way was paved for new standards which could be claimed as a natural result of special American needs and environment.

A force in the American social and intellectual climate which prevailed strongly against the importation of foreign works, except perhaps those of the accepted romantic school, was the moralistic attitude

[52] *The Critical Period in American Literature* (Chapel Hill, University of North Carolina Press, 1951).
[53] *Main Currents in American Thought*, II (New York, Harcourt Brace and Co., 1927), p. 190.

prevalent in all aspects of American life. This moral code is commonly called Puritanism. Bernard Smith points out the danger of this misleading label.[54] Strict moral ideals may not have been derived from the early Puritan settlers. Nevertheless, it was a pervasive and powerful force in literary criticism during a long period of our history and still exerts a pressure. There has been a constant development from a dogmatic and definite application of tests of morality upon literary works to the more sophisticated demand that literature have a moral utility. This was one of the most important esthetic principles of the nineteenth century and many critics expressed the feeling that without moral utility any work of literature could not be justified.

French literature provided an especially fertile field for attack in this respect. It was a generally accepted opinion in the nineteenth century that French literature automatically was to be considered immoral. In spite of this attitude the flow of books from France to this country did not diminish,[55] and this influx was stimulated by the popularity of the romantic school, especially from 1826, when romantic imports from France added their weight to those brought in from England. The acceptance of romanticism in America did not stem the tide of criticism against the viciousness of French writers and the pernicious influence of their works on the morals of American readers. After the middle of the century the trend in France was toward naturalism. This meant that strict moral attitudes were disregarded in order to express unhampered artistic and philosophic ideals of realism. Gilbert Chinard's study of the reception of French literature in the South may be applied just as truthfully to the other regions. He observed that "les préjugés religieux, les jugements hâtifs, les généralisations rapides et fausses, l'orgueil national opposèrent des obstacles presque insurmontables à la pénétration des choses françaises".[56] The fear felt in the East because of the invidious influence of French literature was just as strong as that felt in the South. This is shown in a study of Ameri-

---

[54] *Forces in American Criticism* (New York, Harcourt Brace and Co., 1939), p. 35.
[55] G. J. Joyaux, "French Thought in American Magazines". Unpublished Ph. D. dissertation, Michigan State College (1951).
[56] G. Chinard, "La Littérature française dans le sud des Etats-Unis", *Revue de la Littérature Comparée*, VIII (1928), p. 87.

can magazines from 1830 to 1860.[57] Attitudes toward sexual and social mores as illustrated by certain French authors did not accord with the strong moral code which prevailed in America. These writers were bitterly attacked in literary magazines and critical articles.

Indications that realism was going to be a force in American literature appeared quite early in the century. A growing attitude called for realistic treatment in the novel, which had become the most popular form of literature during the nineteenth century. The demand for a purely American literature indicated a turn toward a realistic treatment which would perhaps have manifested itself without any help from foreign sources. The choice of native settings which could be observed first hand and treated in a careful descriptive manner became more and more an accepted practice among writers.[58] The native American optimism which had supported the romance which characterized most of the literary output was beginning to be replaced by a more observant and materialistic point of view. An anonymous article about current literature in the *Atlantic Monthly* expressed approval of the turn from romanticism and the appearance of Russian, English, German, and French realism.[59]

The change in the intellectual climate of America caused by the exterior forces of economics, social changes, and political events was a gradual one. The demand for an American literature based upon an American inspiration turned the attention of many of the critics away from British literature and toward the native writers who were trying to accomplish this.

The social picture was changing radically during the same period. A growing industrialization accompanied by the movement toward urban settlement created a need for a new picture of life as it really was. Poverty, unpleasant living conditions, and cruel working conditions were evident on every side. Materialism gained as a force in shaping the personality of the common man. Writers could not go on creating an untrue picture of life when they observed the real conditions on all sides, nor would the public be satisfied by a literary production which

[57]   A. Rabinowitz, "Criticism of French Novels in American Magazines". Unpublished Ph. D. dissertation, Harvard University (1941).
[58]   A. Cowie, *The Rise of the American Novel* (New York, The American Book Co., 1948), p. 317.
[59]   See Appendix A, 3.

consisted completely of flights into fantasy and which ignored the true environment in which the reader lived.

Westward expansion served to weaken the influence of the Eastern literary school at the same time that it provided a new outlook on life. The travelers to the West, though many of them may have begun with an idealized picture of their future life, soon were forced to face reality. The lack of physical comforts, the constant struggle they had to wage in order to survive, and the new awareness of the strong forces of nature which often made their efforts more difficult to achieve, all served to create a new breed of inhabitants who were not satisfied with the idealized version of life offered in traditional literature.

The Civil War added to this growing desire for a truthful interpretation of life. In addition to creating a massive upsurge in industrialization with its concurrent social effects, the war afforded its participants an opportunity to see in a raw state the savage impulses to which man is subject. The romantic techniques could only disguise facts which would be apparent to anyone who had lived through the holocaust.

The brutally realistic viewpoint forced upon the American consciousness by the Civil War conditioned the American reader to face other unpleasant truths which were brought to his attention by such books as Mark Twain's *The Gilded Age*. In this book the political corruption of Grant's administration was the subject of literary treatment. This marked a trend in the literature following the War in which the sociological novel employed realistic techniques to call forth critical attitudes toward the social revolution that was taking place in the land.[60] Social novels enjoyed a great popularity. They served the useful purpose of informing the public on important matters. At the same time they provided a realistic and forceful subject matter treated in a truthful manner for those readers who were developing an interest in sociological developments.

All these forces contributed to the decline of the vogue for the historical romance and the gothic tale which was very evident in the 1860's. From 1861 to the 1880's the controversy created by the movement of realism in fiction excited wide interest in the United States. This interest was manifested by a brisk and often bitter discussion of the strengths and weaknesses of the new techniques which filled the

[60]   *Ibid.*, 49.

pages of the literary magazines.[61] The general reading taste was still romantic but was undergoing change influenced by the incipient realism of the regional and domestic novels which had gained vogue. These books, with the depiction of local settings employing observed details, were highly successful. By the 1880's the battle was approaching a climax and needed only the work of a strong champion to triumph over the forces of romanticism. William Dean Howells filled the needed role.[62] He was one of the earliest, and certainly one of the most influential defenders of the realistic techniques. He waged consistent war against the attacks which were appearing with regularity against realism and in defense of romanticism.[63] The critics who favored romanticism believed that realism could not last. They claimed that beauty alone endures from age to age, and beauty was not found in slums. Howells combatted this attitude. He felt that whatever was true, however unpretentious, was always beautiful and good. Goodness and beauty could not reside in a false and unreal view of life. Howells accepted bitter characterizations and sordid descriptions if they were faithfully recorded from real situations. He did not champion immorality, but saw no evil in the descriptions of vice if it were done for a noble purpose. As editor-in-chief of the *Atlantic Monthly* Howells used his influential position to favor the realists. He compared the typical American novel with those being produced in France and found our native product sadly lacking. He left his mark by championing a new trend in novel writing and by aiding in the acceptance of the new school of realism. With his help it was established as the dominant force in American literature by the turn of the century.

Henry James was one of the novelists defended by Howells.[64] He, too, contributed to the defense of the realistic school. At the same time he added to the critical awareness of the values in this school a new dimension which later developed into a broader approach to literary criticism. He drew attention to the importance of form and

---

[61]   V. L. Parrington, *The Beginnings of Critical Realism in America*, p. 288.
[62]   See Herbert Edwards, "Howells and the Controversy over Realism in American Fiction", *American Literature*, III (1931), pp. 237-248.
[63]   See Appendix A, 20, 23, 24, 40, 49.
[64]   E. H. Cady, *The Road to Realism* (Syracuse, N.Y., Syracuse University Press, 1956), p. 152.

esthetic considerations of style. He learned many of his lessons in this respect from Flaubert.[65]

Style and form have never been unimportant in the novel. Since Aristotle form has played an important role in literary creation, and writers have been always interested in the use and function of the correct choice of words. But in the early nineteenth century, form and style were not of paramount interest to the novelist. The romantic school, with its dependence on inspiration for ideas, and its construction which yielded to moods and contents rather than shaped them, was not inclined to allow any limitations to be imposed upon its inspiration because of requirements of form and technique. It was not essential that a romantic work should display tight logical construction and a style which was consistently consonant with the matter being treated. The author intruded at will to elaborate his own ideas or to hold judgment upon his characters and events.

By 1900, realism was firmly established in America. It had not reached this point without bitter recriminations on the part of the supporters of romanticism.[66] And romanticism was not dead, though its popularity had been replaced by that of the new school. America, because of changing social and economic conditions, geographic expansion, internal upheavals such as the Civil War and political scandals, was searching for a new way of seeing and understanding life. Concern with sociological questions and the search for the answers to them, utilizing new standards of morality and new scientific instruments of judgment, encouraged the adoption of the realistic techniques. The most highly thought of works were those based upon this new approach, but others of the romantic and historical schools were avidly read. Romanticism has retained the strength to influence later modes of criticism and writing up to the present day.

The period from 1870 to 1900 was characterized by a tendency to question the current literary trend and by the attempt to discover a new manner which would better express American democratic values. There were strong efforts made to demonstrate that realism must play an important role in forging a native literature and these eventually won out. But in spite of the huge amount of writing in journals and

[65]   See Appendix A, 57, 59, 113.
[66]   *Ibid.*, 42, 48, 49.

books concerning the conflict at the turn of the century, there was surprisingly little in the way of an esthetic or philosophic creed in literary criticism which had been established to guide the critic during this controversy. Charles Glicksberg described the major problems of American literary criticism at this time as the need "to draw up a comprehensive system of esthetics that would at the same time do justice to the structural organization and formal properties of a specific literary work".[67] The criticism of the twentieth century had to contend with an emergent modern spirit, with new forces representing both traditional and untried experiences.

Because of the formless condition of critical attitudes at the beginning of this century, the attempts of American criticism to achieve a standard created a renascence of activity, the final result of which is still undecided. There were in the early decades many currents and countercurrents which represent the differing attitudes of groups of critics. These groups consisted of the humanists, impressionists, social and esthetic critics.

The neo-humanists, as their name implies, demanded a firm standard of scholarship in literary criticism. Historical backgrounds were important to them for the understanding of a literary work. Moral judgment played an integral part in the critical evaluation. The good effects of this policy are obvious. But, carried to extremes, they become pernicious. This is especially true of the moral code.

The moralistic aspects of neo-humanistic criticism were attacked by the impressionists. These critics advocated a development of freedom and a hostility toward what they called puritanism. They discussed European writers, artists, and musicians, utilizing a subjective appreciation and attempting to recreate moods which they claimed to find in the works of their subjects. They discarded almost entirely the historical sense which the neo-humanists found so important. They showed little interest in ultimate values. Their main object of scorn was American provincialism and Victorian morality. Though the vogue for this type of criticism has passed, evaluations based purely on personal impressions are not uncommon and often offer valuable insights.

The neo-humanists' moral standards and classical rules were at-

[67] "American Literary Criticism", *The Western Humanities Review*, VIII (1954), p. 87.

tacked from another direction by Joel Spingarn who, in his lecture on the "New Criticism" (1910), continued along the lines of the impressionists and carried the method one step further.[68] In his essay Spingarn rejected the standard approaches to literature. He admitted that scholarship was necessary to the understanding and elucidation of a literary work, but he decried the moralising attitudes of the neohumanists. Instead, he advocated a more strict attention to the work of art itself. He saw three principal forces which were deteriorating the American concept of literature: the idea of literature as a moral force, the concept of literature as propaganda for a new way of life, and the concept of literature as wholly external to man. This last, he claimed, was responsible for the growth of the ideal of art for art's sake.

Spingarn offered support to a growing tendency toward estheticism in American criticism. By discarding the problems of values he turned the attention toward formal analysis. He rejected the rules of genres, style, metaphor, moral judgment, and history, but insisted upon learning, which facilitated the understanding of the intent of the artist, supported by the added criterion of the critic's good taste. He demanded an education in esthetic thinking, scholarship, and deep sensitivity on the part of the critic. This was a rather aristocratic view of the critic's role in society, but it demonstrated a growing tendency of one aspect of literary criticism. It seemed impressionistic, and Spingarn was accused of following this school because he set forth no clearly defined values. He had thrown out the moral, political, and social standards which help to relate esthetics to human experience. But his tendency toward criticism as analysis of form, showing how the poet fulfilled his intention, led the way to the movement of estheticism in twentieth century criticism.

From 1910 to 1930 a new mode of criticism based directly upon the philosophical-political tenets of Marxism gained strength. The working class became an influential element of society. This new force was often in opposition to the industrialists and professional workers. The socialists, and later the communists, became the spokesmen in literature for this class. The socialist critics emphasized internationalism and realism along with a contempt for gentility. Though they shared some common sympathies and dislikes with the other critical schools, a

[68]   J. Spingarn, *Creative Criticism* (New York, Henry Holt and Co., 1917).

strong Marxist strain was reflected in their critical theory that a work of literature must reflect the author's adjustment to society. In order to understand a work one must understand, and also evaluate, the social forces which produce it. This requirement proved a very limiting factor in Marxist criticism. But at the same time it opened avenues into newer and more valuable modes of criticism.

The Marxist critics, or social realists, continued to be a force in criticism well into the 1930's. Since they employed materialistic criteria with crude simplicity while ignoring esthetic and artistic values, they were open to much criticism from other writers. They admitted that literature may be an instrument of social influence, but the one-sided neglect of its esthetics, as demonstrated by the Marxists, ignored the persistent or timeless quality of a work of art. The social point of view was employed by such critics as Edmund Wilson, Howard Mumford Jones, Lionel Trilling, and Alfred Kazin on a higher and more fruitful level than the Marxists had done. All of these critics were in part sympathetic to the social aims of the material realists, but they were also aware of the esthetic values which must be considered in criticism. They made up the school of liberal critics which developed in the twenties.

Liberalism, which gained strength in the twenties, was not a direct outgrowth of Marxist criticism, but developed alongside it while maintaining common aims. But the liberal critic was more interested in the individual and his role in society than he was in society as a mass. The aim of liberalism was to liberate the artist and enable him to assume the role of spiritual leader in society. The spirit of experimentation and adventure was encouraged. An evaluation of society and culture was called for, but only in order to determine what social pressures of American culture warped, weakened, and hampered the artist. There was also an attempt to utilize that which in past traditions was usable. In 1927 liberalism as a mode of criticism came to full fruition with Vernon Parrington's *Main Currents of American Thought*. Parrington related American literary expression directly to the life and thought which it expressed and underlined the "Americanism" of literature produced in this country.[69]

[69]   R. Spiller, *The Cycle of American Literature* (New York, MacMillan Co., 1957), p. viii.

After the First World War the younger generation demanded more forcefully a rejection of the old standards and searched for its answers in new techniques and methods. Literature was becoming more perfect in techniques and more serious in purpose than ever before. The Marxists and neo-humanists began to give way to a form of criticism which not only dealt with society and personality, but also specifically with literary form.

Dissatisfaction with American social and literary conventions in the twenties manifested itself in a large scale emigration of writers to Paris and other European cultural centers where there was to be found a greater freedom from the inhibiting atmosphere of familiar surroundings. In America there was a strong defeatist attitude caused by the realization that the great war had not really solved any major social problems. In politics socialism was on the wane and money seemed to be the answer and goal of all. In Europe, with its less conservative atmosphere, writers found freedom to protest against the vulgar and materialistic tendencies in modern life and at the same time found new means of expressing the protest. Esthetic experimentation offered a way for the artist to separate himself from the vulgarity of the common mass and at the same time to express his distaste for traditional values and standards to the point where he discarded them almost entirely. In this way he hoped to express more clearly, by means of art, a new set of values for society to accept.

One of the earliest and strongest supporters of the American writers in exile was Edmund Wilson. His book, *Axel's Castle*, appeared in 1931 and provided a creed for young writers as well as a defense for what they were doing. In it he advocated the retention of the historical method but stressed concentration upon textural structure and meaning. He recognized Freudianism, Marxism, and Symbolism as three potent forces at work upon the mind of the novelists of the period. This meant that the critic must recognize the influence of the author's personality, the effects of society, and the role of art in any artistic work.

One of the major techniques of French writing which impressed Wilson was Symbolism. He saw in the use of symbols to express a deeper meaning than the obvious one a manifestation of the author's revolt against society and his attempt to shift his experience of life from an objective world shared with society to a subjective one savored in solitude.[70] Though the use of the symbolistic technique was not new to the American novel, having been employed by Poe, Hawthorne, Melville, Whitman, and Emerson, the device was not one which had been closely observed, or even well understood, by American critics. Wilson explained it and pointed out its importance to American writers and critics. At the same time he defined the importance of semantics. This study was carried even further by Kenneth Burke. Wilson wrote that a literary work induces in the reader a state of consciousness by creating a web of intricate association. This is done only by the subtle and proper use of words with all of their associations brought into play. Words in themselves do not have only pure and definite meanings. They are prime symbols full of suggestions instilled by inflections, pauses, tones, and their order and collocation on the page. Their selection must be such as to bring out previous association.[71] With this in mind, the critic was required to take on a more specialized task and to have an awareness which was hitherto not a part of his technical equipment. The text became an object for close, careful study. This study called for scholarship, experience, and special sensitivity on the part of the critic. It was a major exercise in esthetics as well as an exercise in social and historical evaluations.

The esthetic tradition which assumed a dominant position during the thirties in American criticism derived inspiration from the neo-humanists, the liberals, and the impressionists. Its roots go even further back into the history of literary criticism. The basic ideals stem from the Arsitotelian principles which had been the basis for many critical creeds throughout the centuries. Partly due to the conflicts of the twentieth century schools of criticism, the idea grew up that beauty is wholly a study of expression unrelated to ethics or social philosophy. Although novelistic criticism in the esthetic tradition is almost never achieved in this pure state, the application of the esthetic principle in this century is more intense than it has ever been before. John Crowe Ransom, I. A. Richards, Cleanth Brooks, Yvor Winters, Kenneth Burke, and Allen Tate, among others, have all enriched the tools of the new criticism by the personal application they have given to the technique while holding fast to the essential principle of textual analysis.

[70] *Axel's Castle* (New York, Charles Scribner's Sons, 1932), p. 265.
[71] *Ibid.*, p. 245.

The new critics tended to found the value of literature on art and philosophy. This reaction against historical criticism and the moralistic point of view of the humanists reflects a measure of protest against the ideological tyranny of modern society and the chaos in our concepts of values.[72] Asserting that art is creative and that matter and form are fused in any work of art with the end object of giving pleasure to the observer through his intellectual enjoyment of it, these critics established firmly the principle of textual analysis in order to rediscover and reaffirm the traditional values of literature in a coherent artistic structure. They sought to find the value in the work itself and not in extraneous considerations of sociological, political, economic, or positivistic nature.

Mid-twentieth century American criticism had reached new heights of creativeness and originality. There had been a multibranched growth from the main trunk of nineteenth century critical attitudes and techniques. With the rejection of old standards and the establishment of new points of view derived from the impressionists, the Marxists, the liberals, and the estheticists, there has been a marked increase in the complexity of the critical faculty and a heightened specialization in the function of criticism. This mixture of insights and ingredients has resulted in a rich field, oriented both in the direction of esthetics and the scientifically determined aspects of modern life. Developments and changes in American critical standards during this period of approximately 100 years have been great. When Flaubert first appeared on the American scene with *Madame Bovary*, the realistic-romantic battle was entering its intense period. This first novel, along with his others, and the literary creed they represented have passed through some or all the periods of changing literary attitudes and the critical notices reflect the changing trends. New and changing evaluations of this book have been made depending on the prevailing climate of opinion. Throughout the period from 1860 to the present, *Madame Bovary* has been the only one of Flaubert's works which has been a consistent subject of literary evaluation.

---

[72]   B. Smith, *op. cit.*, p. 349.

III

THE CRITICAL RECEPTION OF *MADAME BOVARY*

In America Flaubert's reception was delayed for nearly twenty years after the publication in Paris of *Madame Bovary*. When in the 1870's his name began to appear in American magazines, the current taste here was for the romantic novel. Later in the 1880's the battle against realism was joined by American critics. As we have seen, the 1890's proved to be the critical years of this struggle. To the American critic of these decades, the French novel, and more particularly the French realistic novel, represented immoral tendencies. For this reason, nearly all of the critical attention that Flaubert received during the 1870's and 1880's was focussed on three major problems: moral values, realism versus romanticism, and the use of art in his technique to cover up the lack of morality in his work.

One of the earliest notices concerning Flaubert which appeared in an American magazine was an anonymous article in the *Atlantic Monthly* of 1862. It brought to the attention of the reader here that Balzac, Flaubert, and Champfleury were using realism to "incarnate in letters nature as it is, without adornings, without ideal additions".[1] No attempt was made in this article to do more than mention Flaubert's name as one of the new school of French writers.

During the 1870's there was more frequent mention made of Flaubert and his work. Most of this notice was unfavorable. Flaubert was classed in the realistic school with no great understanding of his values as an innovator. To him were automatically attributed the faults, which it was felt were part of the traditions of that school. W. P. Morris wrote in 1870: [2] "We question whether a book like *L'Education senti-*

---

[1] See Appendix A, 6.
[2] *Ibid.*, 10.

mentale has never been written outside of France. Many readers will probably add, 'No, heaven forbid!' But it is exactly because we need not apprehend that American authors will go too far in realistic delineation that it is safe to explain what invests books like Flaubert's with their peculiar value and painful fascination." Morris noted that the one thing lacking in most novels was their failure to convince. He felt that Flaubert wrote *Madame Bovary* as a physician would write out a report, coldly and dispassionately. Though he did not relinquish his prejudice against realism, he at least could see some virtue in the technique and the truthful picture achieved by Flaubert's methods. Because of this he termed Flaubert "the perfect type of materialistic poet" who in observation of nature could hardly be surpassed. To Morris he was by no means merely a painter of nature; he was a chemist, an anatomist, a physiologist. "Stones, plants, furniture, works of art, human hearts, – all appear to the author the same", Morris wrote, "and therefore he describes them with the same degree of care, fidelity and indifference. There is nothing omitted, nothing left undescribed."

This grudging admiration for such painful technique demonstrated a basic incomprehension of Flaubert's true method of artistic choice and placement. For this reason the critic felt that "the mirror held up to nature has no focus; the picture it reflects has no conclusion. Where will the realist find a limit if the ideal does not fix one for his guidance?" Morals entered into the judgment. Mr. Morris stated that "in refined society it is not customary to speak of things which an unrefined society will mention without hesitation. Flaubert, it is true, neither praises vice nor condemns virtue, but on the other hand he condemns vice as little as he praises virtue." A writer in *Nation*,[3] however, absolved Flaubert of any guilt as far as producing an immoral work was concerned. For him the moral lesson of *Madame Bovary* was so evident that he recommended it for "young people wavering between virtue and vice". However, this anonymous critic was not a partisan of the realistic school. He wrote, "And yet, we would not for the world have had Mr. Flaubert's novels unwritten. Lying there before us so unmistakeably still-born, they are a capital refutation of the very dogma in defense of which they were written."

The moral question was a concern felt toward most French litera-

---

3   *Ibid.*, 18.

ture. Charles Potvin in the *Atlantic Monthly* [4] offered a partial defense and an explanation for this corruption. He stated that not all French writers were immoral. "Against so sweeping a judgment", he wrote, "the names of half a dozen writers could be mentioned . . . . They are faulty but they are great. Such are Balzac, Georges Sand, and Alfred de Musset." The real root of the evil is, however, a natural fondness of man for forbidden things; "With the French this inclination is hidden within a cloud of pseudo-philosophy. All sorts of foulness are pandered to under the pretense of devotion to art . . . ." Flaubert was considered one of the sinners in this respect. In the regular article about modern French literature which appeared in *Lippincott's Monthly Magazine*,[5] Francis Ashton wrote that "Up until recently French fiction was 'forbidden fruit in America'. People's estimate of the practice of French novel reading was on a sliding scale, which varied from regarding it as a small vice to merely a questionable indulgence. A yellow cover was a suspicious object of discreditable appearance and as such was commonly treated, on the entrance of visitors, – after Miss Lydia Languish's fashion in the *Rivals* – crammed behind the sofa cushions or thrown under the table." He stated that the one major reason given to justify French novel reading is French artistry and esthetics as manifested in the genre. These novels draw life as it is, not as it should be, employing objectivity and considering morals irrelevant. "Among those who profess to describe things as they are", he wrote, "without any sense of sympathy, preference or partiality, the author of *Madame Bovary* deserves the palm." Ashton considered the characters of this novel as sunk in vice and degradation. "Did anywhere, at any time", he asked, "ever exist a group of human beings so numerous, holding such varied relations to one another, with so different natures, yet all like this. If so they were monsters, and the reality of life is no more justly presented by a sketch of monstrous and grotesque deformities than it would be by a sketch of cherubs after Correggio. Yet this book is considered the highest triumph of French realistic art."

This evaluation of *Madame Bovary* seems exaggerated today even to those of a rigid moralistic standard, but it is representative of the

[4]   *Ibid.*, 14.
[5]   *Ibid.*, 15.

attitude of man in the seventies.[6] This seeming lack of moral tone in Flaubert's works blinded the critics of the 1870's to other criteria which were there to be appreciated.

The emphasis that was placed upon the question of morals during the 1870's obscured the more important questions of realistic techniques. The critics felt that immorality was an adjunct to realistic treatment in the novel and their attempts to explain the technique explored only the surface manifestations of treatment of details and the lack of selectivity in their use. During this period the number of articles about Flaubert in American magazines was small and contained very little literary evaluation. No attempt was made to analyze the realistic techniques employed by him. Feeling that a moral lesson should be explicit in any work of art, they blamed Flaubert for not making clear the lesson that people who lead evil lives inevitably end up with a horrible punishment. They felt that Emma's death received such commonplace treatment that the moral lesson was lost. They accused Flaubert of disguising a degraded story under an esthetic treatment. A review of *La Tentation de Saint Antoine* in the *Atlantic Monthly* [7] pointed out that only in the surface technique employed was there any interest to be found in Flaubert's works. The reviewer wrote that:

Flaubert is an author who has won considerable reputation in France by three novels which have already called out a great deal of discussion, both in the country where they were written and elsewhere. They are *Madame Bovary, L'Education sentimentale,* and *Salammbô.* In all of them there is a talent of a certain kind, enough to get itself very much talked about, but chiefly from the novelty of the author in maintaining the paradox that the treatment of any subject, if only cleverly done, can outweigh the most natural objections to a distasteful topic. So much may be said for *Madame Bovary* and *L'Education sentimentale,* at least.

In 1881 the first English translation of *Madame Bovary* appeared in America. During the same year Marcel DuCamp's *Souvenirs littéraires* was published in France.[8] Though the book contained some misleading representations concerning Flaubert's personal life, it did serve the purpose of helping to clarify his literary theories and techniques. In the next year more insight was provided by the publication of Flau-

---

[6]   *Ibid.,* 12, 17, 19.
[7]   *Ibid.,* 16.
[8]   Paris, 1881.

bert's correspondence with Georges Sand.[9] This correspondence gave rise to the idea that there were romantic tendencies which could be discerned in his novels. This impression of Flaubert as a romantically inclined author no doubt aided in his acceptance by American critics who favored that type of novel. Almost immediately after these events a new attitude could be discerned in the Flaubert notices which appeared here. These three publications provided a more valid basis for Flaubert criticism in America.

Howells championed Flaubert's cause in 1881 by calling *Madame Bovary* "one impassioned cry of the austerest morality".[10] A revision of opinion on the part of many critics occurred following the wide dispersion of the English translation of this book and current opinion began swaying more and more toward the acceptance of Flaubert and his method. However, though his prestige was growing, the battle against realism still influenced critical opinion about his works. G. Norton of *Nation* [11] accepted the importance of the author of *Madame Bovary* and admitted his great power as a writer, but he remained highly critical of the school of naturalism which he claimed was founded by Flaubert. He wrote that "Flaubert was a discontented mind without any degree of creative genius or imagination. His horizon of thought was immense, it was boundless, but he had not the faculty of condensing his ideas. We may be sure that Madame Bovary once existed. Flaubert did not create her, he copied her with the exactness of a photographer. All of his other works are a complete failure." We are assured that this critic did read, at least, *Madame Bovary*. Though he perceived nothing in Flaubert's other works which could excite his attention, there was something in the *Bovary* which lifted it out of the "common reality" for him. He wrote as follows, "I remember the impression that *Madame Bovary* made upon me at the time of its appearance. It was not pleasant; it gave me a painful sensation. I was almost ashamed of feeling interested in it: still I was interested."

Three years later in the same magazine [12] Norton elaborated on the romantic characteristics which could be found in Flaubert's work and

[9]   *Georges Sand-Gustave Flaubert Correspondance* (Paris, 1882).
[10]   W. C. Frierson and H. Edwards, "Impact of French Naturalism on American Critical Opinion", *PMLA*, LXIII (1948), p. 1009.
[11]   See Appendix A, 34.
[12]   *Ibid.*, 27, 35.

found that many of his good qualities could be attributed to this influence. In an article of 1882 in the *Atlantic Monthly* entitled "A Note on Flaubert",[13] Henry James wrote that Flaubert was a lyricist and was devoted to the theory of art for art. James considered *Madame Bovary* the best of Flaubert's novels. As for the others, he wrote that "the mass of the public finds them dull". Flaubert's techniques made James wonder how a writer could expend such "an immensity of talent in making himself unreadable. Apart from one's own personal impressions in reading Flaubert, it would be easy to multiply citations from critics to the same effect. Now, as the years go by, it seems more and more certain that of all of Flaubert's works, *Madame Bovary* alone has elements of immortality."

Henry James was one of the most influential in establishing Flaubert as a master stylist and confirming the importance of this aspect in novel writing. *Madame Bovary* was still Flaubert's strongest witness. Two years after his first article James expressed a warmer opinion about Flaubert than he had previously held. In an article on Turgenief in 1844 [14] he recounted a visit to Flaubert and described his interest in the group at an earlier date. He now called Flaubert the "most singular and the most interesting of the group". Turgenief introduced him to Flaubert after having praised the French author highly because of his extraordinary attempts at form and irony. Though James felt that Flaubert had not succeeded completely in all of his efforts, he understood what Flaubert's innovations meant for the form of the novel and concurred heartily in the direction being taken. James wrote of Flaubert that:

He had failed, on the whole, more than he had succeeded, and the great machinery of his erudition and labor which he had brought to bear upon his productions was not accompanied with proportionate results. He had that talent without cleverness, and imagination without having fancy too. His effort was heroic, but except in the case of *Madame Bovary,* a masterpiece, he imparted something on his works which sunk rather than floated them. He had a passion for perfection of form and for a certain splendid suggestiveness of style. He wished to produce perfect phrases, perfectly interrelated, and as closely woven together as chain mail. He looked at life altogether as an artist, and took his work with a seriousness

13   *Ibid.*, 22.
14   *Ibid.*, 26.

that never belied itself. To write an admirable page, and his idea of what constituted an admirable page was transcendent, seemed to him something to live for. He tried it again and again, he came very near to it; more than once he touched it, for *Madame Bovary* will surely live. But there was something unfruitful in his genius. He was cold and would have given anything he had to be able to glow.

James's appreciation of the high achievement that Flaubert had accomplished in style was soon taken over by other critics. It was not long before Flaubert's tedious efforts at perfection of form became a legend in American criticism. Some admired him for it, others blamed the painful process for the coldness that they professed to feel in *Madame Bovary*. The concept of the importance of style over other considerations was felt to be a bad influence on American novelists just as it had been on the French. An article appeared in the *Atlantic Monthly* of 1884 [15] criticizing French preoccupation with style and the narrow view of life which resulted from it. The writer here claimed that "The preoccupation with style is laudable to the highest degree . . . only it is to be feared that with their close Chinese life, their tendency to study the warts rather than the beauties of man, the neglect of the large classes of contemporary life, and above all, their absorbing care of form, the modern French novelists are not getting hold of that large humanity which is alone eternally interesting. The minute and exquisite fineness of their work may end by belittling their brains, until they finally become in literature what the Japanese have become in art; incomparable, if you will, but incomparable in a very narrow way."

During the eighties, critics adopted a more tolerant view of the moral value of *Madame Bovary* perhaps because of the attention they were giving to the literary techniques employed in the novel. Flaubert was no longer for all of the critics merely a representative, or the leader, of the French realistic school. He was cited as an author who taught a valuable moral lesson in his first great novel, and as one who taught valuable new techniques to apprentice novelists. If there were descriptions in *Madame Bovary* which were shocking to the reader unaccustomed to a forthright description of sin, this was necessary to the over-all artistic value of the work and did not serve to glorify the baser instincts of man. Vernon Lee, author of an article entitled "A

15   *Ibid.*, 29.

Dialogue on Novels", which appeared in the *Living Age* in 1885 [16] made one of his speakers say concerning descriptions of sin, evil, and vice, "There is not a single description of this kind which might not most advantageously be struck out, and I would have gone on my knees to Flaubert to supplicate him to suppress whole passages and pages of *Madame Bovary*, which I consider a most useful and moral novel." His partner replied, "I confess I can't well conceive *Madame Bovary* with those parts left out."

In 1885 the eighth volume of Flaubert's complete works appeared in Paris and was reviewed in the magazines in America. In *Nation* [17] Norton wrote concerning the French master's style:

Phrases, pages, in which every word rings true to the thought, stamp on the reader's mind so unusual a clearness and vividness of impression that one can scarcely distinguish it from a spontaneous act of the mind itself. The mingled conciseness and lingering of Flaubert's manner increase the intimacy of sympathy. When he is in the presence of what is familiar, he just glances at it and passes on, speaking only the necessary word to make it visible to us; when he encounters what is peculiar to the moment or the individual, he pauses, watches, gazes intently, listens, and so gazing and listening, delivers those cadenced and magical utterances which create the universal out of the particular, the ideal out of the real, and art out of nature.

The respect felt at this time for Flaubert was evinced also in an article appearing in *The Literary World*,[18] a review of *Salammbô*, which was appearing in the United States after "twenty-five years of neglect". Although the translation was criticized as not being worthy of the original, *Salambô* received the highest praise. The reviewer felt that its influence upon American literature was inevitable. He also reassured his readers concerning his feeling for *Madame Bovary* which he considered a masterpiece and which offered "no blandishment for the evil-doer".

Madame Bovary began to typify those qualities which American critics, who were not satisfied with the novel as it was, felt could add life to the genre. The publication of *Salammbô*, which did not excite the strong attacks against morality and realistic techniques that *Ma-*

---

[16]   *Ibid.*, 36.
[17]   *Ibid.*, 38.
[18]   *Ibid.*, 39.

dame Bovary did, added to Flaubert's popularity in America. *Nation* had contained many unfriendly reviews [19] about *Madame Bovary*. Later it recognized the growth of approval which had begun to appear in critical articles during the eighties. The reviewer for this magazine stated in 1887 [20] that, *"Madame Bovary* remains the type of the modern realistic novel; it has exercised a real influence upon our literature".

Most of the articles concerning Flaubert and his art during this period showed the highest praise. His value to American literature was estimated to be important and he was considered one of the steadiest influences for good in the novelistic art.

Edgar Saltus in 1889 argued for a reappraisal of American fiction.[21] He saw Flaubert as the middle ground between romanticism and naturalism which may safety be trod by American writers. He wrote:

The ambitious writer has on one side of him a corpse still warm, in whose features he recognizes romanticism; on the other is that silk stocking filled with mud which is the emblem of the naturalists. But somewhere near at hand are tombs marked Dostoevski, Flaubert, and Eliot — names that tell all yet nothing save disinterestedness, charity, and the forgiveness of sin. Should the writer hesitate he is lost. Romanticism holds many attractions for the weak writer, its guiles, philtres, and moonlight reveries. Naturalism holds forth the promise of wide publicity and money in the bank. Between allurements such as these many have halted and will halt and conjecture, but presently, not tomorrow perhaps, some hero of letters will brush them aside and pass, with lips austere, straight to the tombs and kneel there and commune. When he arises, it will be with that novel which you and I await.

Henry James, by 1892, expressed a warm appreciation of the work of Flaubert.[22] He saw him now as one of the most valuable masters in the craft of novel writing. He claimed that "Flaubert was a writer's writer as much as Shelley was a poet's poet". James affirmed that one should not confuse an author's personal traits with his art. "Some day or other surely we shall agree that everything is relative, that facts themselves are often falsifying, and that we pay more for some kinds of knowledge than those particular kinds are worth. Then we shall perhaps be

---

[19] *Ibid.*, 24, 34, 36.
[20] *Ibid.*, 44.
[21] *Ibid.*, 46.
[22] *Ibid.*, 57.

sorry to have had it drummed into us that the author of calm firm masterpieces, of *Madame Bovary*, of *Salammbô*, of *Saint Julien l'Hospitalier*, was narrow and noisy and had not personally and morally, as it were, the great dignity of his literary ideals." James wrote that Flaubert should be admired and emulated in his conscious determination to create a work of art. This concept was, as we know, an integral part of James's theory and led to his own unique style. He remarked, "And as Flaubert had deliberately sown, so exactly and magnificently did he reap. The perfection of *Madame Bovary* is one of the commonplaces of criticism, the position of it one of the highest a man of letters dare dream of, the possession of it one of the glories of France."

By the time he wrote these lines, James, as we have noticed, had formulated his theory of the value of esthetics in writing and so was able to appreciate the qualities in Flaubert's other works which were not so apparent to him before. However, he still found in these works the lack of poetry which prevented them from becoming universal masterpieces. His evaluation read: "*Salammbô*, in which we breathe the air of aesthetics, is as hard as stone; *L'Education* for the same reason is cold as death; *Saint Antoine* is a medley of wonderful bristling metals and polished agates, and the drollery of *Bouvard et Pécuchet*, (a work as sad as something done for a wager), about as contagious as the smile of a keeper showing you through the ward of a madhouse. In *Madame Bovary* alone emotion is just sufficiently present to take off the chill. This truly is a qualified report, yet it leaves Flaubert untouched at the points where he is most himself, leaves him master of a province in which, for many of us, it will never be an idle error to visit him."

In 1895 a book entitled *Gustave Flaubert as Seen in his Works and Correspondence* by John Charles Tarver appeared in America and received wide notice. A review of it may be found in nearly every literary magazine of the day.[23] Here Flaubert was firmly and finally established in the public notice as a master of his craft. He was brought to the attention of any who might have missed noticing him before in spite of his wide fame here. In a small number of reviews of this work the traditional puritan attitude is present. Isaiah Smith of *Dial* [24] considered Flaubert's life more interesting than his works. He felt that

---

[23] *Ibid.*, 64, 67, 68, 71, 72.
[24] *Ibid.*, 68.

the average reader had "pushed his way with deepening repugnance through *Madame Bovary* or been awe-stricken but – fatal defect – not interested in the piled-up erudition of *Salammbô*." But even this unfriendly reviewer was forced to pay his respects to the technical and stylistic worth of the books and asserted the weight of their influence upon American letters. E. Newman,[25] a more friendly, but slightly disinterested, critic for the *Fortnightly Review* [26] stated that "those interested in fiction rank Flaubert the highest of all writers". He appreciated the artistic worth of *Madame Bovary*, found that *Bouvard et Pécuchet* is "an important social document and felt that *Un Cœur simple* is the finest of all of Flaubert's stories." D. F. Hannigan in the *Westminster Review* [27] paid homage to Flaubert's artistic integrity and lifted him out of the class of social realism. 'All who look on literature as a precious thing, which is debased by utilitarian considerations, just as gold is by the admixture of alloy", he wrote, "should honor the memory of Gustave Flaubert. In him we recognize the typical artist, whose ideal is the perfection of form, thoroughness of workmanship, and unflinching devotion to truth." H. T. Peck of *Bookman* [28] used Tarver's study to illustrate a point which was of great importance to many critics for the appreciation and evaluation of Flaubert's work. This was the pointing up of his essential difference from the other writers of the French realist or naturalistic school. Frierson and Edwards state that "When in 'Les Romanciers naturalistes' Zola included Flaubert in the group, the implication that Flaubert was a naturalist was flatly denied by the *Literary World*, as it was later by *Nation*." [29]

Peck established Flaubert as the first among the realists. He wrote that, "Mr. Tarver's book is undeniably to be ranked among the most important books of the year in that it throws open to English readers the sources that give a clear and convincing picture of the personality and genius of the writer whose influence is at present paramount in French and English fiction." Flaubert was classed by him as the immediate founder of the realistic school. "It is in Flaubert, therefore,

[25] Some foreign criticism, when it has appeared in magazines or journals which have been influential in the United States, has been utilized in this study.
[26] See Appendix A, 72.
[27] *Ibid.*, 64.
[28] *Ibid.*, 67.
[29] *PMLA*, LXIII (1948), p. 1009.

rather than in any of his predecessors", he wrote, "that we are to find the fruition and perfection of the realistic theory; while the influence of his personal association, as well as of his published works, directed the early labors of Turgenief, Daudet, Maupassant, and Emile Zola." He continued: *"Madame Bovary* is a very striking illustration of the difference between true realism and the excesses of the naturalistic school . . . . In every portion of the epochmaking work Flaubert is seen to be apart from the writers who have abused and corrupted the example of their great master, and who, as has been strikingly said, see only the beast in man, and view humanity as a swarming, huddled mass of growing creatures, each hounded by his own foul appetites of greed and lust." This feeling, on the part of many American critics, of Flaubert's separateness from the naturalists was favorable for his reception in the United States. His moral values, supreme artistry, and disinterested portrayal of truth, gave him a force which was irresistible. He offered small argument to those opposed to the sordid in life, for his esthetic treatment overshadowed the bare reality and transformed it into an artistic creation which presented an implied moral lesson within the framework of a literary masterpiece. Flaubert had an established esthetic system which he followed rigidly and a literary code which was his own. With it he entrenched the school of realism, but, as many felt, his principles were subverted by those who followed him. Though his purpose was artistic rather than sociological, he established a moral tone which was acceptable to American readers while firmly maintaining the role of non-intrusion by the author. His principles permitted him to rule over his material and shape it into an artistic entity which was happily received in America as a model for future writers. At the same time the intellectual and social life in the United States was gradually changing because of the force of events, industrialization, westward expansion, etc., and provided fertile ground for the realistic techniques which had received such wide notice. It is worthy of note that the American reception of the new ideals was selective. Zola with his complete naturalism and outspoken social condemnation was not at first favored, while the tempered realism of Flaubert found a small but enthusiastic group of followers here. In the eighties, a decade before the acceptance of realism, major American critics acclaimed the works of Flaubert. Later, he was, for American critics, the best model which could be found for the writers who wanted to produce a novel which would fill the need felt because of the changing atmosphere in the United States. Flaubert's reception, cold at first, then timid, soon became more hearty when his techniques were exposed and brought into the light. As his works were studied and the worth of them recognized, he became, at the end of the century, the recognized head of the French literary movement, and a writer who exerted a most profound effect upon the art of novel writing.

Early twentieth century criticism tended to follow nineteenth century standards, at least in the first decade. For this reason, though *Madame Bovary* was cited in numerous instances as the epitome of modern novel writing, scattered reviews were published which placed stress on the immoral content of the work.[30] This line of criticism became more influential with the growing importance of the neo-humanists and their emphasis on moral values, though morality never again played the role in the critical notices of *Madame Bovary* that it did during the nineteenth century. The theme has recurred up to the present time. In 1910, a poem written by Clement Wood appeared in the *Greenwich Village Blues.* It reflected both the current, popular attitudes toward *Madame Bovary* and also the contemporary thrill-seeking spirit. It read as follows:

> Way down South in Greenwich Village
> Main Street maidens come for thrillage,
> From Duluth or Pensacola,
> To live à la Flaubert or Zola,
> After each new thrill still racing,
> Rarely chaste and always chasing.[31]

Moral standards have so changed that *Madame Bovary* no longer shocks the sensibilities as it once did. At the same time critical standards have undergone a change. There is a wider separation between morality and art. Modern critics more readily accept Flaubert's ideal of good art being inherently morally good in its effect.

Most of the articles which were about Flaubert's devotion to art and style at the beginning of this century were opposed to the prin-

---

[30] See Appendix A, 86, 88, 89, 95, 96.
[31] Allen Churchill, *The Improper Bohemians* (New York, E. P. Dutton and Co. Inc., 1952), p. 224.

ciple. A few voices were raised in defense. One of the most appreciative of the critics wrote for *Bookman* in 1903 [32] about the stir created by the Extreme Unction scene in *Madame Bovary*. He cited the passage as one of the most marvelous examples for an understanding of Flaubert's creative genius. In order to illustrate the care and discriminating taste which the author had employed to create the passage, five of Flaubert's earlier drafts were reproduced in the article along with an explanation of the scene's development. In the same magazine, a few years later, Emile Deshays [33] related his experience while making a pilgrimage to Rouen in order to relive Flaubert's scenes and meet the people upon whom he had modeled his characters. He found that Flaubert's art was true and perfect so that all that the traveler saw and experienced was already familiar to him through his reading of *Madame Bovary*.

During the first decade of this century James Huneker [34] added his appreciation of Flaubert's works and style, though he did not base it purely upon the traditional or formal tools of critical evaluation. Instead he intuitively applied the criteria of music appreciation in order to arrive at a fervent appreciation of the beauty and harmony which he found inherent in Flaubert's prose. He saw in the French writer the maker of a great style, a lyric poet, who selected as an instrument the other harmony of prose. He called Flaubert the "Beethoven of French prose" and said that a man of lesser gifts, and less exacting conscience, would have calmly written at length, letting style go free in his pursuit of theme. But Flaubert strove ceaselessly to overcome the antinominalism of his material. He wrote *La Tentation de Saint Antoine*, "and its pages sing with golden throats; transpose this to a lower key of *L'Education* and we find the artist maddened by the incongruity of surface and subject. In *Madame Bovary*, with its symphonic descriptions, Flaubert's style was more happily mated, while in the three short tales, he is almost flawless." Huneker wrote that when Flaubert's themes become rusty through the years, it is his music which will live. Through it one will always perceive his "glorious vision of the possibilities of formal beauty that has made his work a classic".

[32]   See Appendix A, 89.
[33]   *Ibid.*, 97.
[34]   *Ibid.*, 92.

This impressionistic form of criticism was attacked by the neo-humanists because of its disregard for any of the formal criteria and its purely subjective application. Above all, it disregarded the moral questions which they felt should be considered in literary criticism. The partisans of the neo-humanist school may account for some of the vehement attacks against Flaubert's adherence to stringent rules of style which appeared at this time. Those who wrote in favor of Flaubert's style did so with disregard for the moral side of their evaluations. At the same time, they represented to a certain degree the growing school of esthetic critics who were basing their critical evaluations almost entirely upon questions of form and style. The neo-humanists were bitterly opposed to both of these trends.

For this reason it is not surprising to perceive in critical notices of the 1910's a great annoyance at the insistence upon the greatness of Flaubert's style and the extreme lengths to which he went in order to achieve it. W. P. James in the *Living Age* [35] doubted the time and effort claimed to have been expended by Flaubert, but said that there had been suffering felt in the creation of his works. This was so because Flaubert could find the right sentence only by writing the wrong one four or five times. According to James, Flaubert had "a critical ear and an unmanageable voice". Another critic, Willard Wright, in 1917,[36] thought that the time had come for a re-evaluation of Flaubert because "the superstition that Flaubert is a transcendent genius has taken so powerful a hold upon the modern critical mind that for one to question his supremacy is to meet with a kind of intellectual ostracism". Nevertheless, he dared to dissent. For him style was not of supreme artistic significance. Inner structure was vastly more important. He felt that Flaubert displayed none. His unprolific output was due to prodigious labor and his characters showed no inner life because of the emphasis placed upon external detail. Wright continued in his analysis by explaining that for Flaubert "the world existed as a model to be faithfully copied, and the reason that his books do not strike us immediately as purely stenographic is that he threw over them a golden and scintillant web of style. His art is therefore to a large extent spurious."

[35] *Ibid.*, 101.
[36] *Ibid.*, 123.

A few attempts to defend Flaubert were based upon the idea of his romantic tendencies modifying the harsh effects of realistic techniques. Some critics still refused to accept the possibility of a great novel being written by purely realistic techniques. They were haunted by the old implication of coldness, heartlessness, and the preoccupation with unpleasant aspects of life. In 1919 a reviewer for the *Living Age* [37] emphasized Flaubert's romantic-realist characteristics. Because of this combination he felt that Flaubert was able to produce *Madame Bovary*, "a masterpiece far transcending Richardson's *Clarissa Harlowe* in its pitiless yet pathetic precision. It is neither immoral nor moral. It neither mocks nor preaches. It is no mere artistic method, still less the photography of Zola. It outdoes Balzac on his own grounds . . . . Contrasted with the simpering *Lady of the Camellias* the book stands as Hogarth to Greuze." This idea was repeated in 1921 by Ernest Boyd who wrote a retrospect of fiction for *The Independent*.[38] He stated that the fame of Flaubert is definitely associated with realism and naturalism which are precisely the elements in contemporary American fiction which are cultivated by the younger novelists. But, he wrote concerning Flaubert's works, "If the author of these books was hailed and denounced as the begetter of the realistic novel, if the Goncourts and Maupassant and Zola elected him as master, later criticism is disposed to regard him rather differently, and to refuse to allow him to be claimed by either the realists or the romanticists. He seems at bottom to have belonged to the latter rather than to the former, but his romanticism is not based upon a horror of reality which is the true mark of the French romantic school."

In spite of this sort of defense the twenties furnish more examples of articles which denounced Flaubert's concept of style than any other period.[39] Though *Nation* continued its defense and praise of Flaubert and his literary theories, it was one of the few magazines which did. Its reviewer wrote [40] that Flaubert's "personality and his work are, in a word that is often falsely but here at last justly used, epoch making.

[37]   *Ibid.*, 128.
[38]   *Ibid.*, 131.
[39]   See James Branch Cabell, *Beyond Life* (New York, 1930), pp. 270-271, for a biting critique of Flaubert's depiction of Emma Bovary written by Cabell in 1919 in his campaign against realism and in behalf of esthetic fantasy.
[40]   See Appendix A, 136.

The modern novel, which is not only a form of art, but a new way of applying human vision to the world, is inconceivable without him."

According to many of the writers of the day, the twenties was a period of intellectual suffocation and puritanical provincialism. Many of the young writers were emigrating to Europe where they could find a free acceptance of experimentation and an unprejudiced appraisal of new artistic techniques. The articles denouncing Flaubert for his unusual emphasis on art in his technique reflect the spirit from which these young writers were trying to escape. J. Middleton Murry wrote [41] that Flaubert's style "is sometimes perfect, sometimes bad, more often indifferent than either". He went on to affirm that Flaubert, because of his fanatical devotion to art, and his detachment from and aversion to life, is a minor and not a major hero in literature. This sentiment was quoted by the author of an article in *Current Opinion*.[42] The title was "Re-estimating the Patron Saint of Modern Realistic Fiction". He wrote that Flaubert did not possess the finest kind of literary discrimination because the use to which he put his unusual visual faculty was primitive. He felt that Flaubert did not know how to employ visual imagery in order to differentiate the subtler emotions of the soul. He also lacked the faculty of metaphor. The author of this article continued by stating that Flaubert showed no depth of vision in his work and lacked inward growth. His vision never deepened, it only became more extensive. In an effort to explain the esteem in which Flaubert was held in spite of his basic inadequacy, he wrote:

What are we to say of a generation that has seen in Flaubert's art the highest achievement in literature, and in Flaubert himself the type of the great writer? Were it not for the fact, the collective hallucination would seem like a chapter in a fairy tale. We can see the cause of the aberration. Flaubert's art is an art which minor writers can understand; in pretending to surrender themselves to it — for a real surrender is much too painful — they have the satisfaction of manipulating a mystery. But the mystification has lasted too long. The invention of art has done no good to art, and it has interposed a veil between Flaubert's work and the general judgement. To be critical of Flaubert is to prejudice a vested interest, so large an edifice has been built upon the insecure foundation.

[41] *Ibid.*, 143.
[42] *Ibid.*, 142.

The publication of Flaubert's correspondence in English in 1921 [43] provided further ammunition for those who opposed his literary techniques. In his letters he had explained in detail his ideas about art and its function in literature. Kenneth Burke [44] used these letters to prove that Flaubert had set himself upon an impossible quest. He felt that Flaubert, who was temperamentally unsuited to the task, was trying, by processes which were primarily intellectual, to write under an esthetic of which the processes were primarily intuitive. The final testimony of the letters, according to Burke, was that he never succeeded in arriving at an esthetic which was amenable to his temperament. A few years later, Gamaliel Bradford wrote in *Harper's Magazine* [45] much the same opinion, although it was arrived at differently. He found the description of the great effort and time which was necessary for the completion of *Madame Bovary* depressing to contemplate. He asserted that this great effort succeeded only in creating a stiff and artificial flavor. He wrote that, "Flaubert left behind him his half dozen books which posterity will prize among its treasures. Yet curiously enough, the very effort of perfection that he lavished upon them seems to make the imperfections stand out all the more. On the other hand, his letters, which he presumably did not work over at all, and which simply welled up from the profoundest depths of his passionate soul, will always remain some of the richest and finest expressions of such a soul that the world has ever seen." He concluded by writing that, "*Madame Bovary* is the triumph of the art, but the letters are the triumph of the artist."

Though the critics of the twenties opposed Flaubert's attention to art, their opinions were unanimous in one respect: they all agreed that Flaubert had achieved a unique place in the art of the novel. Their attacks against the function of art in his technique do not always stand up under analysis. Rather, they often reflect an air of petty refusal to accept Flaubert completely as the majority of Americans seemed to have done. John Middleton Murry,[46] more favorably disposed toward Flaubert in 1924 than he had previously been, tried to explain the

---

[43]   *The Correspondence of Gustave Flaubert* (New York, Boni Liveright, 1921).
[44]   See Appendix A, 138.
[45]   *Ibid.*, 146.
[46]   *Ibid.*, 148.

seemingly uncalled for attacks upon Flaubert's literary creed. He claimed that a poor impression was created by the works of those writers who had tried to imitate Flaubert and only succeeded in creating a parody of his style. Murry described the cult of "flaubartism" which had grown up in the United States, a cult of Flaubert which advocated the literary practices which he himself would have decried. Flaubert was a conscious artist but he was clear and lucid in his writing. It was his followers who created "flaubartism" through the wrong application of his method and their insistence upon hidden meanings in his works. They cultivated a conscious obscurity and called it art. Because of this, many readers who would have enjoyed Flaubert have avoided him as being too deep for them. Murry related that ". . . once he was safely buried the legend was begun. The story of the miracle was read abroad and the ground near the grotto diligently bought up. A thriving trade in literary superstition was created. The art of literature was a mystery; no one could understand it who had not made his pilgrimage to the shrine. Real literature was incomprehensible; if it was not incomprehensible, it was not real. Naturally, the common man, accustomed to going to literature as a life-giving delight, left Flaubert strictly alone." Murry also explained the extravagance of "flaubartian" practice in the United States by the materialism of modern civilization. The reaction against it was extreme. Flaubert appeared in America as a savior, "for an act of homage to him is the only possible protest". The wide sale of Flaubert's books in translation here contradicts Murry's contention that the common man was afraid of Flaubert because of his reputation for deepness.

The unfavorable attitudes toward Flaubert's ideals of art were carried on into the thirties before they lost their intensity under the barrage of critical writings extolling his contributions as discerned by the esthetic school of criticism. Burton Rascoe was one of the last bitter critics. He indulged in a contest with Arthur Maurice in the *Bookman* in 1927 [47] over the constant use of the term, *"le mot juste"* as it was being used by contemporary writers. He did not object to its application in Flaubert's works, but he did resent its use by others who could lay no claim to the practice. Later, in 1932,[48] Rascoe attacked Flaubert

[47]   *Ibid.*, 160.
[48]   *Ibid.*, 171.

most severely on the grounds of morality, art, and technique. He wrote that, "The gabble about Flaubert's search for *'le mot juste'* became a persistent dogma among the esthetes, ... Alongside these legends about Flaubert's search for the exact word (which he could have found if he had asked the postman or the cook) there grew up other absurdities – absurdities so great that it is a wonder that any mere common reader ever dared to pick up one of Flaubert's sour romances and pursue it with pleasant enjoyment to its always conclusive end." He stated that:

Flaubert did not write artistically, his dispassionate appearance was due only to the division between romanticism and fact, between acceptance of bourgeois life and the fashionable intellectual revolt against reality ... Nevertheless, despite all that has been written about his dispassionate artistic attitude, it (Flaubert's self) was there in the character of a chilly, unsympathetic, unfeeling moralist, his mind, which is to say, his intellectual judgement, in fee to the 'correct' intellectual attitudes of his time, always triumphing over what he felt in his heart.[49]

The articles which appeared in the nineteenth and early twentieth centuries in the discussion concerning the application of art in Flaubert's work, for the most part, showed the same lack of critical discrimination that those concerned with morals and realism did. They cover approximately the same period of time, though those concerned with style began later and extended further into the twentieth century, being especially notable during the twenties. But the concern manifested in these articles seems today a shallow one. The concept of style had not reached the degree of technicality that it has in our times. When the critics wrote of form, *le mot juste*, correct use of details, and the other canons of writing as practiced by Flaubert, they were describing only exterior manifestations of style. Only James seemed aware of the importance of style and form as an integral and interwoven part of the whole work of art. With the general apearance of articles in the forties and fifties, written by critics who applied the criteria established by the school of esthetic criticism, a more complete and valid appreciation of the importance of Flaubert's principles concerning art and literature developed. Then it became clear that his attention to art was not a mere extension of the romantic retreat into art for art's

---

[49]   *Titans of Literature* (New York, G. P. Putnam's Sons, 1932), p. 379.

sake. Rather it was a genuine attempt to extend the craft of novel writing in new directions. it demonstrated Flaubert's belief that art must be made an integral part of the creative effort in literature just as it was in music and painting. The textual analysis which this direction in literary criticism called for showed up two aspects of Flaubert's craft which had previously remained relatively unnoticed. One was the extensive use which he had made of symbols, the other was his superb interior form and structure obtained by his attention to esthetics in his artistic creation.

Nearly all of the articles discussing Flaubert's use of symbols appeared in the 1950's. It is surprising that a book such as *Madame Bovary*, which had aroused so much interest, been studied for so many years, been the subject of so much discussion, and which made such clear-cut use of symbols, had not until this time been noted for its symbolistic technique. Many of the articles which have recently appeared treating this aspect of Flaubert's art, and all of them use *Madame Bovary* as the major example, have been excellent. Through them new insights have been gained into Flaubert's intentions and meanings. They have shown that he consciously used the symbolistic technique in a regular and coherent way as part of his method to develop moods and meanings.

Alfred Engstrom was one of the first to write of the symbolism employed in *Madame Bovary*.[50] He pointed out that

The exquisite style and concentrated form of *Madame Bovary* have made Flaubert famous as an artist in French fiction. But it is neither the style (in the usual sense of the word) nor the narrative form that makes the work so memorable. It is not even the character of Emma, though she is remarkable of her kind. As Henry James, who was still fascinated by her, observes, Emma herself does not touch upon enough life to be humanly representative – nor does life touch enough upon her. Yet there is something there which links *Madame Bovary* with the great imaginative tradition.

Engstrom found that this link is the symbolic use which Flaubert made of irony. The great themes of the book, over and beyond the immediate treatment of provincial life, are love (or more precisely, the search for love), boredom, fatality, and death – with a vast pattern of irony as a solvent for all the other elements. Engstrom, by

[50] See Appendix A, 217.

bringing this to the reader's attention made possible a far greater understanding and enjoyment of the descriptive passages and the action
of the novel. For example, Charles Bovary's school boy hat represents
to the perceptive reader a complete picture of his background and
character. The garden scenes become meaningful when related to the
action of the story. Background details and scenes all add to the mood
and ironic meaning which the tale unfolds. It becomes evident that
Flaubert did not employ irony simply because it was natural to his
temperament. He used it consciously as a literary technique. When-
ever it appears, irony is utilized as part of a major pattern designed to
bring out insensibly the themes of the work in an artistic way.

R. Blackmur in the *Kenyon Review* [51] pointed out how the character
of Emma Bovary has taken on added dimension with the symbolistic
approach to the study of the novel. She has represented, during most
of the years that the book has been in circulation, a dissatisfied woman
set in uncongenial surroundings. Her fate has shown up the tragedy
that unbridled passion and disregard for social standards can bring
about. But in recent years she has even achieved, with her double aspects of beauty and inherent psychological weakness, the status of a
major symbol of life. Her beauty, which is out of place in her surroundings, combines with her inability to accept the reality of her situation to represent the necessity of both good and evil in life.

Partisan Review [52] published an article by D. van Ghent entitled
"Clarissa and Emma as Phèdre", which also treated Emma as a major
symbol and compared her creation to that of Clarissa Harlowe. Since
both characters are creations of different times and periods of artistic
development, the author wisely did not attempt to make a comparison
on stylistic and technical points. But he did find that the comparison
of the two characters as versions of love-myth was illuminating inas-
much as they both, one ingenuously, the other ironically, give the universal voice to modern idealism. They both give dramatic form and
religious significance to the same mass of aspirations, attitudes, customs, and passions. The author felt that the myth of Clarissa Harlowe
conformed naïvely to that acquisitive idealism which has been morally
rationalized by Puritanism and afforded a religious depth of fear,

[51]   *Ibid.*, 226.
[52]   *Ibid.*, 223.

perverted sensuality, and death worship. The myth of Madame Bovary conforms deliberately to the archaic mode and is centered in the ancient, tragic, religious intelligence of the value and destructibleness of life. The myth is given precise temporal dimensions by its modern setting in a culture which denies both the value of life, and with irrational logic, its destructibleness. He ended with the statement that, "when life is denied it cannot really be destroyed for it is already destroyed".

William Tindall [53] explained the deeper significance and more universal interest to be found in the symbolistic structure of any work.

When we read a symbolistic novel for the first time or even the second or third, we may find it slight or even naturalistic. When we read it again, however, we find that the concrete particulars and arrangement which gave us that impression are there to carry meaning beyond immediate significance; and as we proceed, a greater meaning gradually emerges. Each rereading adds fresh discoveries, changing our idea of the world until we despair of reaching the end of that suggestive complexity.[54]

Approaching Flaubert's works with this in mind, Tindall found that "ignorant of what Melville had done a few years earlier, Flaubert reinvented the symbolistic novel. Some have confused him with realists and sociologists, but he detested realism and loathed photography with Baudelarian passion." [55] He felt that this was undeniably Flaubert's conscious aim. He composed his novels in a poetic frame. Tindall quoted a letter in which Flaubert said that his method "is a way of perceiving external things, a special organ which sifts matter and which, without changing it, transfigures it". He sought a style "as rhythmic as verse, as precise as the language of science, and with the undulations and modulations of a violoncello". Thus he discarded analysis and commentary and made concrete, evocative or intrinsic details assume their function. He was carried away by the idea and desire for pure art which was later to tempt Mallarmé. Flaubert dreamed of a novel about nothing, without exterior connections, held together by the internal force of style and expressive by form alone. In *Madame Bovary* one can see a step in this direction. Details, rather than the

[53]   *Ibid.*, 249.
[54]   *The Literary Symbol* (New York, Columbia University Press, 1955), p. 71.
[55]   *Ibid.*, p. 73.

author's comments, create the impression. Tindall pointed out how Emma's first arrival at the house of Charles Bovary is replete with detail. Her impressions are not analyzed or commented upon. Instead we see her act, enter, go upstairs, notice her predecessor's bridal veil, stare out of the window. Her own veil, through which she observes her bourgeois surroundings represents her blue, romantic haze. After the ball, Emma found a cigar case, which represented to her the male, distant and aristocratic. Throughout the story Binet's lathe is used symbolically to evoke a feeling of crisis. Emma's most important emotional crises are attended by the sound of this machine, which, going round and round, endlessly turns out useless objects. The reader is never made aware of the sound as an essential, contingent part of the scene, but it is always there below the threshold of awareness representing by its motion, humming, and pointlessness the futility of Emma's life.

Louise Dauner in an article, "Poetic Symbolism in *Madame Bovary*",[56] made a close and detailed analysis of the use to which Flaubert put symbols in his work. She, too, mentioned Binet's lathe. Another major symbol which she found used throughout the work is that of the garden. She saw this as a dominant symbol representing Emma's gradual disintegration of emotion and character. It is also a sexual symbol. She pointed out its first use when Emma rearranged the garden as the new mistress of Charles's house. By this means one is made aware of her incipient romanticism and of her desire to eradicate the first wife by her burst of energy and initiative. Later, in her disillusionment, she went out into the garden to recite romantic verse. At the ball, when Emma glanced out into the garden, its image brought back to her mind pictures of her early life. The final garden scene, in its desalution, mirrored her complete disillusionment. The sexual connotation is brought out by the fact that all of her trysts with Rodolphe were kept in the garden setting. Miss Dauner affirmed that, ". . . one of the major achievements of this novel lies in its superb use of symbolism. Here too the novel moves into the realm of poetry; for poetry as indirect statement, must depend largely upon the use of symbols, and much of the aesthetic and even moral interest of *Madame Bovary* lies in the symbols: those elements in the narrative which

[56]   See Appendix A, 252.

communicate so richly values over and above their literal meanings." She found that Flaubert's symbols are deeply rooted in the nature of their surroundings and are a natural outgrowth of his observations put to artistic use. They are not subjective or esoteric and are easily comprehended into the whole, always becoming a natural part of a given situation or instance.

Interpretation of Flaubert's work by symbolistic meaning has brought to light much that had previously gone unobserved. The reader has obtained through it a deeper and wider understanding of the meaning of the novel. The logic and coherence of the use which Flaubert has made of symbols demonstrate that they are no accident of style but have been employed consciously in such fashion as to add depth and dimension to the surface meaning of the book.

The more recent critical notices by the modern critics who emphasize technique and textual analysis are not limited in their evaluation of *Madame Bovary* to its symbolism. The so-called "new criticism" has been one of the most potent forces for keeping Flaubert's name before the public eye in the last two decades. His theories of the craft of fiction are in accord with the tenets of this school, and the practitioners of esthetic criticism have utilized his works to demonstrate the validity of their techniques. His belief in non-intrusion by the author, the value of art in the creative process, the rejection of traditional appurtenances in the novel, and the concept of the union of form and idea, all developed while writing *Madame Bovary*, are fully in accord with the most recent critical standards. From their studies of Flaubert's first novel, modern critics have produced a fruitful harvest of interesting literary evaluation. The infinite patience which he employed in writing his books so that every word, every phrase, every sentence, every part would fit perfectly into the context afforded a good subject for the careful textual study which is favored by the modern critic. The result has been a vigorous reaffirmation of Flaubert's eminent place in the field of novel writing.

It was not until strict textual analysis was an established fact in American criticism that this type of study made a significant appearance. Henry James had indicated in his appreciation of Flaubert that his artistic tendencies were his most important contribution to novel writing. But the majority of the critics did not really understand all of the implications involved. In 1927 Ludwig Lewisohn,[57] speaking of Flaubert, stated that the American novel, which is not only a form of art but a new way of applying human vision to the world, was inconceivable without him. Lewisohn affirmed that the works, "which transcend the noises of their day, from *Esther Waters* to *Of Human Bondage* and from *Washington Square* to *Main Street* owe the character of their innermost being to Flaubert".[58] He felt that the French novelist's greatest contribution was the modern concept of the infusion of art into the craft of story writing. He wrote that Flaubert "saw that moral power and spiritual significance inherent in the material, in the personal vision which is identical with style, and in the interpenetration of those two".

Not all of the practitioners of the new criticism found Flaubert's dedication to art agreeable to contemplate. Alan Tate [59] agreed that Flaubert achieved the necessary poetic power to create a whole and complete impression of life. But he did so unwillingly. He wrote, "Gustave Flaubert created the modern novel. Gustave Flaubert created the modern short story. He created both because he created modern fiction. And I don't like to think Flaubert created modern fiction because I don't like Flaubert." He added, "It is through Flaubert that the novel has caught up with poetry." Though he does not clearly explain his dislike of Flaubert, Tate is forced by his critical sense to admit that it was the French novelist who for the first time consciously and systematically taught the modern writer how to put completely the imaginative essence into the novel with total texture of scene, character, and action.

The esthetic point of view has been most widely used in recent years by the critics who have reappraised Flaubert's works, and especially in the treatment of *Madame Bovary*. The articles which have appeared have been numerous.[60] Caroline Gordon has pointed out the misapprehension on the part of early critics as to the important aspects of Flaubert's novels. In her article, "Notes on Faulkner and Flaubert",[61] she demonstrated how successful Faulkner was in following Flaubert's ex-

[57]   *Ibid.*, 158.
[58]   *Cities and Men* (New York, Harper and Bros., 1927), p. 163.
[59]   See Appendix A, 205.
[60]   *Ibid.*, 229, 232, 235, 238, 240, 244, 248.
[61]   *Ibid.*, 214.

ample of creating the union of concrete historical detail with lyricism. Both authors have been most successful in combining the inner and the external structure of their books in order to give a complete impression of life. Kenneth Burke concentrated on the verbal aspects of Flaubert's art, as has been pointed out, and found that he was correct in restraining the tendency in his nature toward expansive verbal expression, though he was made unhappy by so doing. Percy Lubbock worked from yet another angle and discovered a novel usage which has made *Madame Bovary* the most effective book for teaching the craft of fiction. He was especially interested in Flaubert's use of distances to portray the complete character of Emma. By using different points of view and distances Flaubert was able to create effects showing the various aspects of her moods and personality.[62]

Georges Poulet was also interested in distances as part of the internal structure of *Madame Bovary*. In his article "The Circle and the Center",[63] he pointed out that in this novel the milieu is a vast surrounding space spreading from the center point, which is Emma, to an indeterminate circumference. From the circumference interest is redirected back to the consciousness of the central character. Poulet supported his thesis by bringing to our attention numerous uses of the circle image in all of Flaubert's works and in his correspondence. He wrote that "For the first time in the history of the novel human consciousness shows itself as it is, as a part of a core, around which sensations, thoughts and memories move in a perceptible space."

These articles illustrate the richnes of material that has been found in *Madame Bovary*. Critics, influenced by esthetic critical standards have not found the novel devoid of suggestion for fresh and interesting analyses.

For the centenary of the publication of *Madame Bovary* in 1957, Martin Turnell [64] wrote a re-evaluation of Flaubert in the light of modern critical reviews and the development of the opinions that his work has aroused. Turnell felt that the study of Flaubert's novels in the light of modern emphasis upon textual analysis, symbolism, and struc-

---

[62] "The Craft of Fiction", *Essays in Modern Literary Criticism*, ed. R. B. West, Jr. (New York, Rinehart and Co. Inc., 1952).
[63] See Appendix A, 248.
[64] *Ibid.*, 267.

ture added to the prestige which should be accorded the French novelist. He claimed that Flaubert was a writer with serious weaknesses who has always divided the critics. His work also arouses strong partisan feelings. If much of the criticism of his novels has been off the target, or has been concentrated on their content instead of their method, Flaubert himself is not free from blame. His correspondence has often misled or misdirected the critics into unprofitable discussions. But Turnell felt that there was a need to assert Flaubert's claim to the title of the greatest virtuoso who ever practiced prose fiction. He was the creator of the contemporary novel, and the source of nearly every technical advance made since the middle of the last century. The pre-Flaubertian novel was primarily concerned with narrative. His predecessors were concerned with a succession of events in time which constitute the relation between the novel and reality. "In *Madame Bovary* the meaning lies rather in an elaborate network of interrelated images which all reflect the coloration or the nuance at which the author was working", Turnell wrote. "Symbolism as utilized by Flaubert meant the substitution of an image for a direct description, or for a description of feelings. His images were usually visual." This usage had perhaps instinctively occurred in writers previously, but Flaubert, he suggested, exploited its possibilities consciously and systematically. Turnell continued, "I felt inclined to describe Flaubert's influence as 'decisive', but the right word is 'seminal'. It was essentially creative because it enabled writers whose natural endowment was superior to Flaubert's to realize their potential to the full."

Turnell showed in his review how completely Flaubert satisfied modern standards of fiction by his internal fusion of imagery and meaning which makes up structure. For Turnell, Aerol Arnold, and other critics to whom structure is fully as important as symbols and textual study, Flaubert was a master craftsman. That Flaubert provided in *Madame Bovary* a perfect example of solid internal structure was testified to by Arnold in his article, "Why Structure in Fiction: A Note to Social Scientists".[65] Arnold complained that too many "specialists" have examined literature, paying no attention to form and structure, seeing only content. However, form and structure are necessary to the full meaning of a work of art. Arnold wrote that this belief

[65]   *Ibid.*, 270.

is due to Flaubert and Henry James who in inventing the modern
novel made it essential that in fiction the arrangement of the material
should suggest its meaning. There were to be no diverting little
episodes, interesting in themselves but addding nothing to the mood
or meaning of the narrative, as in the novels of Fielding or Dickens.
The novel that Flaubert and James invented moved away from history
toward poetry and drama. Arnold pointed out that long novels have
a great variety of scenes and must have some variety of moods, but if
they are to be considered as art objects, they must, like poems, have a
dominant theme or a controlling idea to which everything in the book
is related. They must project a dominant mood. If one opened *Madame
Bovary* at almost any spot, Arnold claimed, by reading a chapter or
even a portion of a chapter, one could see the essential structure of the
novel. Chapter after chapter develops the theme of the contrast between
dream and reality, between hope and disillusion. He wrote that "As we
move from scenes to the novel as a whole, we realize how action following action leads us inevitably to accept Flaubert's conclusion; that the romantic Emma sees not the world outside, but her own dreams; the romanticism is self-deception and that the self-deceiver becomes the
deceiver of others; that finally the deception destroys the romanticist
and also those closely related to her. But how much more do we learn
of the nature of man from this novel! We learn that most people live
in a world of illusion, and that man understands very little of man. . . ."

   In 1957 V. Mercier [66] listed in retrospect the reasons for Flaubert's
lack of success in the novel. According to him, it has been impossible
to find a central treme in any of Flaubert's works. Because of the impartiality of the author, all of the elements in the novels have equal
importance. He also found it difficult to discover any emphasis because of the author's impressionistic style. Through his excessive research Flaubert obtained details which he used merely as details giving
them no imagistic or symbolistic import. Mercier felt that Flaubert was
a hoarder of facts, of himself, of things. Finally, he was not a morally
great person and the reflection of this is seen in his works. This article sums up the salient facts of most of the adverse criticism which
Madame Bovary has received over the years. In spite of the opposition
of this sort which it has faced from some of the critics in America,

[66]   *Ibid.,* 263.

the examination of the critical material which has been published up to the present time shows that *Madame Bovary* is emerging brighter in prestige and literary worth.

Flaubert's great novel has had a long public life in the United States. The critical notices it has received naturally mirrored the important critical standards of the various periods. The notices which appeared in the sixties and seventies of the last century showed only the prejudices which were current concerning French literature generally and the realistic school in particular. They were unfavorable because French literature had a poor reputation in this country. At the same time, critics were aware of the encroachments that realism was making here. *Madame Bovary* provided a good focus of attack as the representative of this new school. Nevertheless, there were a few defenders of the novel who could perceive the invigorating force which it might provide in American writing.

In the eighties, the battle against realism and immorality continued in American critical writing. But the publication of Flaubert's novels here, though they did not still the opposing voices, did afford fairminded critics the opportunity to judge his works more objectively and at first hand. The result was that *Madame Bovary* was soon cleared of the charge of immorality, and was recognized as possessing literary values which were uncommon here and needed in the American novel. By the nineties, Flaubert was firmly established as the foremost technician of the novel who was at the same time a good moral force in literature. He was considered an innovator who could teach our novelists much about the craft of fiction. Reviews of his work, for the most part, showed good critical judgment based upon more valid standards and criteria.

The establishment of Flaubert's reputation in America was closely linked with the establishment of realism in the novel here. Since he represented, in the minds of Americans, those techniques which were necessary to realistic treatment in fiction, and since his position was so high in the literary field, *Madame Bovary* was a potent factor in the struggle for acceptance of realism in the United States.

One must not ignore the other factors, of course. There was a growing tendency here toward the use of realism in fiction. Political, social, and economic factors all helped to determine the direction of literature toward this end. Many American writers were experimenting with the technique and they were abetted by prominent critics. But only in *Madame Bovary* was there to be found the complete illustration of the realistic ideals being formulated during the period. And this book became popular with the public as soon as it appeared here. It was the object of numerous articles in literary magazines. It was soon accepted as one of the greatest classics. Flaubert, with his pronouncements concerning methods of writing fiction, crystallized the ideas which were being formulated in America. He demonstrated the validity of these ideas by his novel *Madame Bovary*. In this way, his example helped to establish realism as the dominant force in American fiction at the turn of the century.

In the twentieth century, in spite of the established reputation of *Madame Bovary*, voices were still being raised in protest against the work. This protest took mainly the form of an attack against the emphasis placed upon the values of art in the techniques found in this novel. Those who made this protest felt that complete adherence to artistic principles in writing induced an aridity and coldness in the finished product. There are still those who feel this way. But the protest was invalidated to a degree by the fact that it represented also a sociological manifestation. In the twenties the neo-humanist critics were opposing experimentation in literature. They considered artistic innovations a form of evasion and escape, which they were. For this reason, some critics opposed Flaubert for this aspect of his writing, whereas, in another time, they might have been able to appreciate it. This was shown to be true later in the century when estheticism became a formula of literary criticism.

Madame Bovary has held the interest of critics in the twentieth century because it has provided a good source for their modern ideals of critical evaluation. Liberalism and estheticism have been the main forces in the intellectual formation of modern literary criticism. The liberals have not emphasized the importance of *Madame Bovary* as an expression of the modern mind. But the partisans of the esthetic school have given the book much study. They have discovered in Flaubert an early symbolist. They have found in his work and in his critical statements many of the seeds from which grew the methods which they employed in their studies.

Madame Bovary received important critical attention in the United States over a period of eighty years. Because of the controversial aspects of its literary innovations and the truthful, unadorned picture of humanity it painted, the novel has been both damned and praised. Flaubert, as the author of the much discussed book, gained a widespread reputation as a writer of significance. For this reason, the works which followed *Madame Bovary* were received in America with great interest and expectation. Those critics who expected another book of the style of *Madame Bovary* were disappointed. *Salammbô*, which followed *Madame Bovary* after six years, was unrelated to it in content and form. For this reason its reception in the United States has followed a pattern different from that of *Madame Bovary*.

IV

SALAMMBÔ, LA TENTATION DE SAINT ANTOINE, AND TROIS CONTES

The early reviews in the United States of *Salammbô* and *La Tentation de Saint Antoine* usually appeared together either in a treatment of Flaubert's work as a whole or in a study of *Madame Bovary*.[1] Though these books were not as severely criticized here as was *Madame Bovary*, any early praise they received was feeble. Neither of the books enjoyed a large reading public in the United States until their English translations became available. The early reviews show the same lack of comprehension and critical standards as did those of *Madame Bovary*.

In 1874 a reviewer for the *Atlantic Monthly* [2] wrote a criticism of Flaubert's realistic techniques. He disapproved of them. He cited *Salammbô* and *La Tentation* as two later works which demonstrated clearly Flaubert's lack of writing ability. He did not classify either of the works as realistic. Quite the contrary. He wrote that "*Salammbô* was an attempt to breathe life into the few fragments that we have left of Carthaginian history, and it labored under the misfortune of being, even when carefully done, hardly more than a *tour de force.*" *La Tentation* he found even less comprehensible. It did not even have the dubious distinction of being realistic in technique. He added, "If Flaubert meant to be realistic, he could not succeed without having much more imagination. The liberties he takes are enough to convict him of error in the field of antiquity; for instance, was Hilarion a neoplatonist? Is it within the limits of possibility that such visions could appear? Has the book any dramatic interest, in other words? We think this can hardly be claimed." In spite of the evidence of massive research, careful literary techniques, and intellectual exercise, this critic

[1] See Appendix A, 10, 11, 14, 19, 22, 24.
[2] *Ibid.*, 16.

found nothing but cleverness in Flaubert's work, and felt that it left the reader little improved as cleverness always does.

Salammbô was first published in English translation in 1885.[3] *La Tentation* did not have a widespread public here until 1910 [4] when Lafcadio Hearn made his translation of the work. Immediately after the appearance here of the *Salammbô* translation the book received more specific attention and more intelligent consideration. At this time, *Madame Bovary* had attained a certain measure of respectability and this was evident in the reviews of *Salammbô*. At the same time, realistic techniques in this novel were not so obvious to the untrained eye of many nineteenth century critics and it was considered safe to praise *Salammbô* which had not acquired the stigma of immorality that *Madame Bovary* had suffered. In 1886 the reviewer for *The Literary World* [5] warmly greeted the book which had appeared "after twenty-five years of neglect". Though he felt that the translation did not do justice to the original, he considered the publication an important one because of the inevitable influence which he felt it would have upon American literature. *Critic* published a review which was not enthusiastic. Its reviewer read the book "with some strong emotion, but very little avidity'. He felt that very few people would be interested in it at all. However, many readers were interested in the book. Its popular appeal before the turn of the century almost equalled that of *Madame Bovary*. It was printed in five editions here. This popularity was maintained until the 1940's,[6] partly because of the obvious artistry of Flaubert's technique. The book's unusual setting and subject also helped maintain public interest. The vastness of the setting and the events obscured the careful realistic treatment of details. The plot was exciting and exotic and served as an escape from life rather than as a means of studying human needs and emotions.

Flauberts mastery of style in *Salammbô* did not go completely unnoticed, however. The reviewer for *Dial* [7] described his careful research

---

[3]   *Salammbô*, trans. M. French Sheldon (New York, Lovell, Coryell and Co.).
[4]   *La Tentation de Saint Antoine*, trans. Lafcadio Hearn (New York, Alice Hariman Co.).
[5]   See Appendix A, 41.
[6]   See Appendix B for editions of *Salammbô* published here during this period.
[7]   See Appendix A, 40.

and painstaking efforts to create a stylistically perfect novel. He wrote that, ". . . the result of all this labor, it is surprising to say, is not a piece of pedantry or a labored mechanical construction, but a work drawn on the broad and symmetrical lines of art". He added that he turned with little pleasure from "the strong meat of such works as these to the pastry of home-made fiction". *Salammbô* made him feel a painful sense of the limitations of American authors.

Henry James, when he wrote of the mastery of Flaubert's style, included an appreciation of *Salammbô* and *La Tentation*.[8] He found them completely praiseworthy in this respect, though lacking the spark of creativity which made *Madame Bovary* a masterpiece. He wrote that *Salammbô*, in which "we breathe the air of esthetics, is as hard as a stone; . . . *Saint Antoine* is a medley of wonderful bristling metals and polished agates, . . ." James approached these works from the esthetic point of view and did not mention other qualities which might distinguish them. These two works were taken more or less for granted by other critics and cited as interesting examples of Flaubert's art which were important stylistically, perhaps, but which did not merit the analysis and study which had been given to Madame Bovary because of its artistic perfection and completely realistic technique.[9]

In 1951 the idea of Flaubert's romanticism was revived. *Salammbô* provided the source for this effort to take Flaubert from the school of realism. Lewis Piaget Shanks wrote an article entitled "The Romanticism of Flaubert",[10] which appeared in *Dial*. In it he discussed ideas taken from a recent collection comprised of articles by F. A. Blossom, "La Composition de *Salammbô*", P. B. Fay and A. Coleman, "Sources and Structure of Flaubert's *Salammbô*", and A. Coleman, "Flaubert's Literary Development".[11] Making use of the great amount of research done by these writers, Shanks pointed out that all of Flaubert's early literary influences were romantic. All of his early unpublished writings were indeed romantic in inspiration and conception. *Madame Bovary* and *L'Education* represented a conscious break from romanticism, Shanks declared, but the other works, especially *Salammbô* and *La*

[8]   *Ibid.*, 57.
[9]   *Ibid.*, 39, 43, 45, 47, 55.
[10]   *Ibid.*, 119.
[11]   *Elliott Monographs*, ed. E. C. Armstrong (Baltimore, The Johns Hopkins University Press, 1915).

Tentation, were completely romantic in every respect. In them Flaubert had given free rein to his romantic tendencies, to lyricism, and to imaginative conception. Those who claimed to find realism in the works were misled.[12]

Lafcadio Hearn [13] was also one who felt that *Salammbô, Trois Contes*, and *La Tentation* were the only works which truly represented Flaubert's real genius. Hearn had done a masterful translation of *La Tentation* which has remained the definitive English version of the work. His evaluation of Flaubert's books was impressionistic and highly subjective, but Hearn displays a genuine feeling and appreciation for the beauty of the three works which he considered Flaubert's greatest. He wrote that he would have preferred for Flaubert to have followed his natural tendencies and not to have been influenced by DuCamp and his other friends. Hearn thought that Flaubert was a unique manifestation of genius with no parallel in history. He wrote that "Romantics and naturalists have both claimed him as belonging to their antagonistic schools; but the truth is that Flaubert belonged to no school; that he did not even found a school – for he will ever remain inimitable – that he followed no system, obeyed no particular literary canons, and sought only the strange and the beautiful wherever he could find them. More especially the strange – the marvelous, the weird, the exotic – the beauty that is barbaric, the charms that are savage." Hearn had a strong liking for these very qualities as evidenced by his interest in Oriental literature. His particular viewpoint enabled him to appreciate *Salambô, Trois Contes*, and *La Tentation* more than he did the works which are usually considered the masterpieces. He was attracted to the blaze of color and the freedom of inspiration and composition which he professed to detect in these works. He was not aware of the fact that they were written just as carefully and composed with just as much attention to style and form as were the *Bovary* and *L'Education*. He did not believe that these two latter works revealed Flaubert's artistic powers.

Though the critical reaction to *Salammbô* and *La Tentation* was not strong, the frequent publication of the former indicates that there was a favorable reaction on the part of the reading public. Perhaps the

---

[12]   See Appendix A, 107, 110, 112, 115, 117.
[13]   *Ibid.*, 145.

exotic settings and local color attracted some readers. There is much in the book to hold interest and attention, vivid descriptions of dress and customs, and battle scenes impressive in the vastness of their conception and the excitement of their action. The novelty of the subject and the excitement engendered in many scenes by their realistic treatment can be cited as an explanation for the popularity of the book with the public while the critics seemed unimpressed in general.

La Tentation did not enjoy a large reading public. It repeated Salambô's exoticism, vivid colors, and strange settings, but its intellectual content did not have the popular appeal of Salammbô. The limited number of editions of this work which have appeared in the United States would indicate that La Tentation has never captured the public imagination. But there have always been readers who have been able to find in it a marvelous depiction of a contemplative subject drawn with consummate style.[14]

The collection, Trois Contes, which contains the three stories, Hérodias, La Légende de Saint Julien l'hospitalier, and Un Cœur simple, has received no greater notice here than did Salammbô and La Tentation. Almost from the beginning, however, Trois Contes has enjoyed a high rank in both public and critical esteem.

The American reception of this book has been, with the exception of a few early notices, just as warm and as undisturbed by adverse criticism as it was in France. It appears that neither Trois Contes nor any of the single stories it contained were brought to the attention of American critics until the publication in Paris in 1885 of the eighth volume of Flaubert's Œuvres complètes, by Quantin. The reviewer for the Atlantic Monthly [15] was not unduly impressed by this latest work. He knew of Flaubert as the leader of the French realists and this fact colored his judgment of the volume. Ignoring Hérodias and Saint Julien, he concentrated his attention on Un Cœur simple as an example of the mistakes inherent in the realistic technique. He wrote that, "In the first of these tales, Un Cœur simple, he [Flaubert] makes a study of a servant woman, but, after all, the reader cannot help asking if it is not work misapplied. What Flaubert shows is how much more observant a realist he is than the sort of woman the old servant was.

---

[14]   See Appendix B for American editions of La Tentation de Saint Antoine.
[15]   See Appendix A, 43.

Insignificant details are crowded into every page, but simply for their own sake; when they are all in the tale ends, and the reader is left to admire or not to care for, as his nature may direct, a rather cold-blooded study of an ignorant, kindly old woman." Considering the predisposition of American criticism at that time against realistic techniques, this review is not surprising. But a determination to find nothing admirable in any work written by Flaubert is evident.

G. Norton in *Nation* in 1886 [16] was more fair-minded and showed evidence of having given the work a careful reading. He had written the previous year that he had blushed with shame at finding *Madame Bovary* interesting. In 1886 he wrote, "If it can be said of a reprint, we should say unhesitatingly that few more interesting books of literature have appeared last year or will appear next year than this final volume of Flaubert's works just issued by Quantin." He continued: "It is the only volume of the eight which could be put, by one who cares for Flaubert, into the hands of one who had not acquired a regard for him with strong confidence that the general impression would be agreeable."

Trois Contes had for this critic a valuable lesson to teach in style and in morality. It represented what was highest in the writing of fiction and did not have the distractions of immoral implications which occurred in Flaubert's other works. By the nineties, many critics who could not accept all of the praise which *Madame Bovary* had occasioned from its partisans were willing to pay honor to *Trois Contes*. They often picked *Un Cœur simple* for special praise, and it was cited as Flaubert's greatest work.[17] Of the three stories, this is the one which has remained an enduring favorite in America. From the turn of the century to 1920 *Trois Contes* had eight editions in the United States. In the thirties there were five, and in the forties, three. Interest has dropped in the stories as a group, but *Un Cœur simple* has reappeared many times in college and high school textbooks as an illustration of Flaubert's realistic techniques. It is short and compact and makes a useful, perfect example of the power of his style. Unfortunately, too often the work is misinterpreted by teachers and used as proof of Flaubert's pessimism and misanthropy. They point out the old serv-

[16]   *Ibid.*, 38.
[17]   *Ibid.*, 64, 67, 68, 72.

ant's tireless, devoted, and unrewarded service as typical of Flaubert's view of life. When dying, she mistakes the bedraggled, dirty,
stuffed parrot for the symbol of the Holy Ghost, and this is pointed
out as an example of Flaubert's supreme irony. Such was certainly not
his intention. He stated in his correspondence that he wrote *Un Cœur
simple* as a work of love. He depicted a life of unselfish devotion and
service and this life was the sole reward for one whose reason for
living was the desire to serve.

Salammbô and *Un Cœur simple* have enjoyed some degree of popularity in the United States. But critical notices would not indicate that
they, along with *La Tentation de Saint Antoine*, *Hérodias*, and *La
Légende de Saint Julien* have made a great impact upon American
critical opinion. Of this group *Un Cœur simple* alone seems to have
stood the test of time as indicated by the enduring respect that it has
been accorded by critics and students of literature.

V

L'EDUCATION SENTIMENTALE AND
BOUVARD ET PÉCUCHET

L'Education sentimentale and *Bouvard et Pécuchet* were the last of all of Flaubert's works to receive critical attention in the United States. These two books were the most difficult of any that he wrote for the nineteenth century mind to understand and appreciate. Their composition represented a deliberate attempt at literary innovation, the purpose of which escaped the intelligence of early critics. It was not until the 1930's that both of these novels received the acclaim and the critical analysis which they deserved. Both works pose problems which have troubled the consciousness of present-day intellects. These problems are beginning to be more fully understood. Flaubert's two novels revealed the conditions which framed man's involvement with the positivistic spirit and developed the consequences of it.

The victory of positivism in France occurred in the latter half of the nineteenth century. Auguste Comte had tried to demonstrate that the only method for the acquisition of knowledge was the scientific method. Comte advocated a meticulous observation of the facts of nature and a systematic interpretation of these facts in terms of cause and effect. One could thereby arrive at an accumulation of results which make up a mass of practical knowledge. The complete application of this method had the result of invalidating any meaning which was separated from causes. In effect, the inner meaning of anything which was unmeasurable and unobservable was ignored and man thereby began to lose the ability to know his human self or the meaning of his environment. Spiritual values were considered intangible and therefore unknowable. In the twentieth century positivism developed into logical positivism or linguistic analysis. The attempt to give a scientific validity to all aspects of life led to the belief that all language is mean-

ingless unless it communicates the facts of actual events which observation or experiment can confirm or disprove. In this manner, man
was dislocated from nature. All of his utterances were considered
meaningless unless they were based upon measurable qualities. Inner
meanings were ignored for exterior forms which could be observed
and noted. For example, moral judgments, which have no factual
references, became meaningless.

Positivism has been a valuable method of scientific research. By
means of it man has learned much about nature and how to control it.
But the more he learns to master nature, the less he seems to understand the meanings of life. The latter half of the nineteenth century
was dominated by science and positivism. This spirit entered into
every aspect of human conduct, literature, and philosophy. Some literary critics instinctively recognized the consequences of this in literature and waged an ardent battle against realism which was a manifestation of positivism. Flaubert was a master realist. But he also knew
that in order to utilize the new spirit in literature it must be controlled
by art. He knew that man could begin to read the meaning of nature
only when, instead of merely copying or describing what he sensed,
he began to comprehend it as a series of images symbolizing concepts. He recognized the importance of the imagination as a means of
apprehending the outward form of things as the image and symbol of
their inner meanings.

Flaubert was aware of the implications that positivism held when it
was applied to human activity as it was in the nineteenth century and
as it has continued to be applied in the twentieth. He wrote *L'Education sentimentale* to describe a society which was imbued with positivistic principles and values. He utilized the realistic techniques which
he had developed, and this realism was an illustration of the inner
meaning to be found in the book. He used details and observed facts
as the structure and form of his novel. But the whole is put together in
such a way as to impart an inner meaning. The significance of the
whole, articulated from that of each part, chapter, sentence, word, appears by itself in sharp outline. Unfortunately, this meaning was not
apparent to the nineteenth century reader.

Flaubert tried again with *Bouvard et Pécuchet* this time trying by
means of satire and humor to make his message clear. Again he failed.

Now, with the opportunity that twentieth century man has had for retrospect, these books present an important truth. The twentieth century has tried materialism and science. American philosophers are again searching for new ways in which one can live in a world of science and retain the spiritual values he needs. Interest is turning to books such as *L'Education sentimentale* and *Bouvard et Pécuchet* in which the reader today may begin to understand the implications of the society which he has formed and in which he must live.

L'Education sentimentale was published in France in 1869. It was semi-autobiographical, for Flaubert based the central character, Frédéric, on himself. The Schlesingers, whom he had met as a child in Normandy, were the models for the heroine, Marie Arnoux, and for her husband, depicted in the novel as a successful publisher. All of the events in the book reflect the activities of the period, and current political and social happenings provide the background for the story. In general, it is life in France in the middle of the century which is the setting against which Flaubert placed the relatively less important activities of his protagonists. The subject of the book is the frustration and lack of direction which a sensitive and ineffectual young man felt in a society which was materialistically oriented. Flaubert here repeated the theme of *Madame Bovary* in which the individual, because of psychological and intellectual traits, is unable to cope with his environment and is ruled by it. But *L'Education sentimentale* was wider and deeper in its scope. The setting was not a provincial town but Paris, the cultural center of the nation. Currents and influences from the outside world were here also keenly felt. Whereas the passing of time in *Madame Bovary* is not an integral theme of the work, in *L'Education* the reader is made aware that he has passed through a whole era in French history. And during that time, the conflict between idealism, as exemplified by Frédéric, and the materialism of the period come clearly to the fore. Every detail, event, and turn of style was a conscious attempt on the part of Flaubert to show this conflict.

One finds in this book romantic manifestations of a spirit in revolt against the materialistic philosophy of the day. Art is used as a means to provide a basis of compatibility between the two. Even more than *Madame Bovary* it provides a masterful example of perfection of technique in fiction.

When *L'Education sentimentale* was published in France it was not liked by the critics or the public. Contemporary readers were too close to the events being depicted to be able to perceive the meaning of the whole. They were living in an age characterized by the intellectual and spiritual attitudes which Flaubert portrayed in the work and they were unable to see in the book anything else than a dull, truthful delineation of their every-day surroundings and their every-day activities. They were satisfied with life as they found it and were not aware that Flaubert's novel gave a prophetic picture of the influence which their society was exerting upon their spirit. The work so perfectly reflected the society and history of the period that the artistry which accounted for the picture was not perceptible to them. It was both a critical and a popular failure.

Another factor which might account for the disinclination on the part of literary men to praise the work was the political significance which it held. When *L'Education* appeared in France, literary censorship was still in effect. The tone of the work was not sympathetic to the intellectual conformity demanded by the political regime in power. Kenneth Burke wrote that the book was so redoubted for its treatment of political issues that of the one hundred and fifty persons to whom Flaubert sent complimentary copies, only thirty dared answer him.[1]

In America the book was received with as little enthusiasm. The most important reason for this was the long period of time which elapsed before there was an English translation available. *L'Education sentimentale* was mentioned in reviews of *Madame Bovary* or *Salammbô* and in articles about Flaubert and his methods. But no attempt was made to analyze the work or explain it to the public. Not until the 1930's did it generate the interest that Flaubert's other works had. In 1870 W. Morris wrote an article on realism [2] which attempted to explain the peculiar value and fascination that *L'Education sentimentale* held for the American writer. The fascination that Morris discovered was that of the unrelieved application of realistic principles. But the characteristic trait that he perceived in most of Flaubert's novels was their inability to convince.

His opinion is typical of that expressed by the reviewers who were

[1]   See Appendix A, 138.
[2]   *Ibid.*, 10.

interested enough to write about *L'Education*. The first English translation of the work which was available to the general public was published in New York in 1922. It was competently done by Dora Ranous
but created no stir in critical circles. As late as 1927 most of those who
had read the novel echoed Hearn's critical evaluation.[3] He wrote that
L'Education,[4] first written in 1845 but not published until 1870 because the author felt the necessity to rewrite and revise it, was unreadable. He called it the only one of Flaubert's novels which could justly
be called a failure.

Only one among the earlier critics valued what Flaubert had accomplished in this great novel. Huneker,[5] with his impressionistic approach
to literature, was enthralled by the brilliant style and construction of
L'Education. At first he got the impression of looseness of construction, but this vanished on the second reading. He expressed himself
as follows: "Almost fugal in treatment is the development of episodes
and while the rhythms are elliptical, large, irregular, rhythm there always is — the unrelated, unfinished, unrounded, decomposed sem-
blance to life is all the while cunningly preserved. The whole book
floats in the air; it is a miracle work. It is full of the clangor and buzz of
time's loom." This judgment is to Huneker's credit for it caught the
feeling and purpose of the novel more closely than any other American critic had yet done. When American readers began to realize the
greatness of the work, it was the supreme artistry of construction, on
the one hand, and the vivid re-creation of an historical era on the
other, which captured their imagination.

Harry Levin in 1948 [6] was struck by the mastery of style displayed
in *L'Education sentimentale*. He called Flaubert's technique of fusing
content, detail, plot, and background into a living evocation of the
past, impressionistic. By using this technique Flaubert was able to
capture every aspect of life, embodying in the story characters and
backgrounds, the very essence of the spirit and consciousness of the
period which he was describing. Levin attributed the lack of appreciation of Flaubert's complete genius to previous critics' misapprehension

---

[3]   *Ibid.*, 142, 143, 150.
[4]   *Ibid.*, 145.
[5]   *Ibid.*, 92.
[6]   *Ibid.*, 215.

of this art. He pointed out the historical background which had been covered in the story, the end of romanticism with the July Monarchy in 1830, the literature of social consciousness which began to appear in the forties, the swing to the right with the revolution of 1848, and the intellectual wasteland which ensued following the *coup d'état* of 1857. Flashbacks carry the reader back to 1805. The central plot of *L'Education sentimentale*, however, takes place within the years 1840 to 1851. Levin pointed out that Flaubert, without interjecting personal comment, made his reader feel the effects of the destruction of the nobility in 1789, the middle class in 1848, and the people in 1851. One can agree with Levin that the novel is indeed, as its title suggests, a moral and sentimental history of the men of its time.

Levin wrote that Flaubert's protagonist, Frédéric, was not immoral nor flabby, as Henry James suggested, but merely subject to all the contradictions and disillusionments of an illusion-ridden age. His hero was foredoomed to failure because of the time and place. His part called for indecision and ineffectuality because Frédéric's position was a false one. Paris dominated the book rather than the actors in the story. According to Levin, it was "not the flagrantly romantic metropolis of Balzac but a more subdued, more subtle, more poetic vista. To render the great city with all its noises rustling around the heroine like an orchestra, Flaubert utilized every artistic medium."

Levin urged the reader to approach the book in the following manner:

Step back and squint: the ugliest negations of his subject assume a positive beauty of composition; the most embittered controversies dissolve into a mood of esthetic contemplation. The term "impressionist" would not be current until Monet exhibited his "Impression: Sunrise"; but members of that school were gathering at Batignolles when Flaubert published his book, and it constantly reminds us of them: of Pissaro when Frédéric strolls down the boulevard, of Manet when he joins his friends at a cafe, of Monet when he observes reflections in a river, of Degas when he takes Rosanette to the races, of Renoir when he kneels at the feet of Madame Arnoux.

Levin claimed that it was not until Joyce's evocation of Dublin that it was demonstrated anew how the wanderings of the modern citizen may be charted against the divagations of the city.

Esthetic criticism of this century opened the doors to a valid appreciation of the artistry inherent in the construction and form of *L'Education sentimentale*. For the first time an author had consciously attempted to depict, in terms of one man's spiritual and intellectual development, the life of an era, while at the same time utilizing the general philosophic and social attitudes of the period to explain his hero's predicament. Since the setting was vast and composed of intangible suggestions of intellectual and political movements as well as physical details of background, Flaubert's choice and arrangement of details had to be made with supreme artistry and subtlety in order to convey the encompassing mood of the period which would convey a physical feeling of life and participation. Flaubert achieved this in his novel.

Paul Goodman illustrated in his study of literary structure [7] that *L'Education sentimentale* is the perfect example of modern novelistic plot and structure where action and events are replaced by ideas and moods. His criteria recall Flaubert's ideal of the perfect novel about nothing in which nothing happens. Goodman claims to have discovered this tendency in the modern novel: an absence of dramatic sequences compounding into a conclusive climax. Today novelists are interested in ideas more than in events. They analyze intellectual and emotional development in terms of every-day life. By examining the inner structure of *L'Education* Goodman has been able to point out its conformity to the novelistic pattern as he sees it. In it personal history parallels political history, and everything goes from bad to worse and arrives at nothing. It has well defined action that remains novelistic in that it does not compound into dramatic scenes. There is full development of sentiment and character and yet no development of plot in the traditional sense.

In all of the modern critical evaluations of *L'Education* one is made aware of the insistence upon fusion of structure and content. It is this achievement which has had the greatest appeal to the American critic of recent years.[8] It was evident in *Madame Bovary* and helps to account for the esteem in which that book is held. The technique is greatly expanded in *L'Education* and illustrates the panoramic effect which may be obtained by it. At the same time, the novel satisfied another

[7]   *Ibid.*, 240.
[8]   *Ibid.*, 242, 243, 245, 250, 260, 270, 274.

requirement of modern literary critics. It contained a message of serious sociological implications. The liberal critics of this century have discovered this meaning, which was not obvious to earlier ones, because it discusses a problem which has become most troubling in recent years. Because of mass media of communication the pervasive effect of materialism has been rapid and extensive. The problem is more immediate in America than it was in France when Flaubert treated it in his novel. The basic aspects remain the same. Flaubert's view of man and modern culture has struck a responsive chord in the minds of many who have experienced the disillusionment and discontent with the direction taken by American society and culture.

Ezra Pound was one of the earliest to remark about the link between Flaubert's mind and that of modern, twentieth-century man.[9] He wrote that, "More and more we come to consider Flaubert as the great tragic writer, not the vaunted perfect stylist. I mean that he is the tragedian of democracy, of modernity." He pointed out that Flaubert, by using generalization and by avoiding the anecdotal and the accidental, has in each of his four works on contemporary subjects created a portrait of man in general as subject to his environment. Nothing that any of his characters could do would alter their case. Pound concluded that "America needs a Flaubert to generalize and register the national folly without a tender hand".

In a letter to Louise Colet, Flaubert had recognized the obligation of the artist to concern himself with human problems. He asked, "What is the artist if he is not a triple thinker?" Edmund Wilson used this phrase as the title of his book about socially conscious writers, among whom he included Flaubert.[10] Wilson reminded the reader that for decades Flaubert had figured as the glorifier and practitioner of literary art at the expense of human affairs, public and personal. His estheticism, nihilism, and consecration to the search for the "*mot juste*" have all been studied and explained. His admirers have tended to praise him for the same things that have caused his critics to find him sterile and empty. Wilson wrote that, "Really, Flaubert owed his superiority to those of his contemporaries, Gautier, for example, who

---

[9] *Ibid.*, 140.
[10] *The Triple Thinkers* (New York, Harcourt Brace and Co., 1938), pp. 100-122.

professed the same literary creed, to the seriousness of his concern with the large questions of human destiny." Wilson felt that in his interests Flaubert was almost as close to Michelet, Renan, and Taine, as he was to Gautier and Baudelaire. He quoted from the letter to Louise Colet Flaubert's criticism of Taine and Sainte-Beuve because of their complete preoccupation with the social aspects:

There is something else in art besides the milieu in which it is practiced and the physiological antecedents of the worker. On this system you can explain the series, the group, but never the individuality, the special fact which makes this person and not another. This method results inevitably in leaving talent out of consideration. The masterpiece no longer has any significance except as an historical document. It is the old critical method of La Harpe exactly turned around. People used to believe that literature was an altogether personal thing and that books fell out of the sky like meteors. Today they deny that the will and the absolute have any reality at all. The truth, I believe, lies in between the two extremes.[11]

Wilson saw Flaubert as a great idealist. He believed that there were great forces in humanity which the present was suppressing and which might some day be set free. He pointed out that Flaubert wrote as follows: "The soul is asleep today, drunk with the words she had listened to, but she will experience a wild awakening in which she will give herself up to the wild ecstacies of liberation, for there will be nothing more to constrain her, neither government nor religion, not a formula; the republicans of all shades of opinion seem to me the most ferocious pedagogues with their dreams of organizations, of legislations, of a society constructed like a convent." Wilson stated that *L'Education sentimentale* has not been truly appreciated because Flaubert's social analysis has been ignored.

Modern criticism has demonstrated the fact that there is a deeper meaning to Flaubert's novels than is apparent on the surface. Recent critics have appreciated the manner in which he has constructed his great novel, *L'Education*, so that the meaning appears in the whole and pervades every part. It is this aspect which has given the novel greater popularity in the last three decades than it had ever enjoyed before. In a review of the second translation of the book entitled

---

[11] See E. Wilson, "Flaubert's Politics", *Partisan Review*, IV (1937), pp. 28-35.

"Sentimental Education Today",[12] one reads that, 'The most important book to be published in English in 1941 was the first intelligent translation into English of Flaubert's *L'Education sentimentale*.[13] It is now acknowledged to be Flaubert's masterpiece, a profound and sardonic comment on his own generation and the France of his youth. It is in every way pertinent to the human and social dilemmas of our own day."

When Flaubert realized that the public and critics did not understand or appreciate what he had attempted to do in *L'Education sentimentale*, he left the theme for the time being. But the problem of man in modern society was a pressing one for him, and he was determined to try to express his viewpoint again. The second attempt, *Bouvard et Pécuchet*, was the book he was working on when he died in 1880. It had been completed, but its companion piece, or final part, *Le Dictionnaire des idées reçues* was not. *Bouvard et Pécuchet* was published in the year of Flaubert's death. The message was essentially the same as that of *L'Education*. Form and setting were entirely different. Flaubert attempted in this book to utilize humor and satire in order to make his meaning clear. He also developed to a greater degree his theory of the novel about nothing in which nothing happens. He chose as his central characters two men, one tall and lean, the other short and fat. They both represent the modern day Candide who would like to find the answers to his questions about life and how it should be lived, but who ends up knowing no more than when he began.

Bouvard and Pécuchet tried to find their answer to the question of how to live an adjusted life in modern society by going to the authorities. They suffered from the common error of their time in having supreme confidence in the authoritative voice or the printed word. They put everything that they found in books to the test, not in an effort to disprove but because they were incapable of living without guidance. Nothing stood up to the test. All of their authorities failed. Bouvard and Pécuchet did not despair, they simply changed their vocation and searched out different authorities. After making numerous endeavors in every field of knowledge, they decided that they were hopeless and returned to their original occupation as copy clerks. They

[12] See Appendix A, 201.
[13] Trans. A. Goldsmith (New York, 1941).

were never embittered, but always naïve and likable. The rest of their lives was devoted to copying aphorisms and bits of knowledge culled from books and authoritative treatises written by famous men.

The book was unsuccessful when it was published. The humor escaped all but a few critics, and the meaning was hidden to those who suffered from the same delusions as the two protagonists. In America it was just as grossly misunderstood. Not until 1954 was an effort made to translate the book into English.[14] Before this translation was made, reviews of the work were infrequent. Those which did appear accused Flaubert of the usual faults of misanthropy and pessimism. The critics in America were just as incapable of seeing the humor in the work as were their earlier French counterparts. In 1892 Henry James wrote that the drollery of *Bouvard et Pécuchet*, "a work as sad as something done for a wager", was "about as contagious as the smile of a keeper showing you through the ward of a mad house".[15] Hearn was able to perceive the comic elements of the work but was not left with a happy impression.[16] He wrote that, "Bouvard et Pécuchet, the most horrible satire on human folly ever written since the days of Jonathan Swift, is worth reading, and if read, it can never be forgotten. Though no book was ever more funny to read, no book was ever written which leaves so sad an impression upon the reader." It is difficult to understand how the humor of *Bouvard et Pécuchet* has escaped the attention of most of the people who read the book. The sad impression that it left was felt perhaps because Hearn and others were susceptible to the meaning behind the work and were disturbed by it. But the happy ingenuous character of the two old protagonists of the work, and their sly and humorously ironical commentaries on both the people and the knowledge which they encountered during their adventure in country living, are infectious. Flaubert did not create in this work a morbid and bitter picture of human stupidity, but rather presented to the reader a warmly sympathetic laugh at humanity's weaknesses and foibles.

The humor in the work is brought out in a variety of ways. Girdler

---

[14] *Bouvard et Pécuchet*, translated by T. W. Earp and G. W. Stonier (Norfolk, Conn., New Directions, 1954).
[15] See Appendix A, 57.
[16] *Ibid.*, 157.

Finch studied all of Flaubert's works and found in them indications of a predisposition to the comic effect.[17] In 1940 he wrote that the comic element pervades Flaubert's work though it is not always evident. The union of the comic and the tragic, for Finch the mark of great literature, is seldom found as fundamentally united as it is in Flaubert. Utilizing the Bergsonian definition of the comic, Finch saw in all of the works the necessary struggle of the soul with the body, of the ideal with its limitations, of beauty with vulgarity, of thought with form, and of fluidity with rigidity. He gave instances of comic juxtapositions in *Madame Bovary*, *L'Education sentimentale*, *Bouvard et Pécuchet*, and even in *La Tentation de Saint Antoine*. These included mechanical stiffness versus vital humanity, physical senses overwhelming the soul, material aspects of an occupation implying poverty or absence of an ideal, multiplicity of aspects juxtaposed in a comic manner, faillures to distinguish relationships and values, disguises, attention to the physical in questions of moral nature, and the insertion of absurd ideas into the mold of sacred ideas. The application of these principles may be observed in Flaubert's works, as Finch pointed out. It is unlikely that the reader would find them funny in his serious novels. They do serve the function, however, of underlining the tragic or serious effect that Flaubert aimed at. In *Bouvard et Pécuchet* the whole spirit of the book is comic. These devices employed by the author add to the humor and multiply the effect of dislocation which one can observe in the two main characters.

More important to modern critics than the humor is the picture of modern man and his tendency toward intellectual and spiritual conformity that Flaubert has drawn in *Bouvard et Pécuchet*. Frank Marzials wrote in 1903 [18] that Flaubert's misanthropy destroyed much of the good effect brought about by his literary artistry. He considered *Bouvard et Pécuchet* Flaubert's revenge on humanity. In it Marzials found a mass of evidence to verify the author's nature which showed "not so much a pure hatred of mankind as a terrible love for studying the seamy side of human nature. Stupidity, dullness, had for him an immense attraction. He gloated over things base." Ellen Fitgerald con-

[17] *Ibid.*, 197.
[18] *Ibid.*, 90.

curred in this evaluation.[19] Though she had reservations as to Flaubert's greatness, she had made a pilgrimage to Rouen in his memory. She, too, felt that his misanthropy was in a way answerable for the partial failure which she discerned in his art. "It would be a pity", she wrote, "if Flaubert should never learn that it was his scorn for the simple things of life that made him a triumphant craftsman instead of a great interpreter of men and women." Yet it was Flaubert's insight into the mind and spirit of nineteenth century men which makes *L'Education sentimentale* and *Bouvard et Pécuchet* so meaningful to us today. His craftsmanship is important, for no great insights attract interest unless they are presented in terms which will arrest the attention. But conversely, no great art, if it is empty, can maintain enduring interest because of its virtuosity alone.

Lionel Trilling has given a lucid and valuable insight into the meaning of *Bouvard et Pécuchet* and the importance which that meaning has held for the society of the nineteenth and twentieth centuries.[20] He pointed out that the novel is a reaction against the ideological aspects of these societies. In the nineteenth century it was characteristic of the novelist to express the idea of society as a definite external circumstance of the individual life. *Bouvard et Pécuchet* added to this awareness by the intelligence it imparted of the part that is played in modern life by ideas, not merely assumptions that have always played a part in every society, but ideas as they are formulated and developed in books. Trilling wrote that the originality of Flaubert's perception lay in its intensity. Others before him had been aware of the role of ideas in shaping character, but in *Bouvard et Pécuchet* books themselves assume the virtual role of *dramatic personae*. It is they which constitute reality for the two heroes. Through this extravagance Flaubert signalized the ideological nature of modern life. Trilling pointed out that:

Bouvard et Pécuchet stands for the condition of life of any reader of this book, of any person who must decide by means of some sort of intellectual process what is the correct theory of raising his children, or what is the right principle of education; or whom he should be psychoanalyzed by — a Freudian, a Reichian, a Washingtonian; whether he needs religion and if so, what confession is most appropriate to his temperament and

[19]   *Ibid.*, 102.
[20]   *Ibid.*, 250.

cultural background; what kind of architecture is best suited to his life style; how he shall feel about the State; the Church; about Labor; about China; about Russia; about India. If we try to say how the world has changed from, say, two hundred years ago, we must see that it is in the respect that the conscious mind has been brought to bear on almost every aspect of life; that ideas, good, bad, indifferent, are the essence of our existence. That is why Flaubert was made rabid by his perception of stupidity.[21]

In the light of modern criticism any view of *Bouvard et Pécuchet* as a manifestation of Flaubert's misanthropic nature loses credibility. In this story his animus against the bourgeoisie was not savage. His characters which represented the conflict were not horrible, they were simply comic. The true villain of the piece was the Idea. All of the failures of the two heroes came about because of the weaknesses of the ideas which they followed rather than because of weakness in their character or physique. The genuine comic nature of the two protagonists and the train of events of the story softened any pessimism which may have crept in. Bouvard and Pécuchet were not imbeciles, as is commonly asserted. If they were, the comic effect would soon have turned to horror. They had character and differing natures. They also had the common fault of wanting to learn too quickly. They came into conflict with the ideological nature of modern life and were laughed at because they did not conform to the ordinary image and stereotype of the roles which they attempted to play. They did not represent the bourgeoisie. They were in conflict with the influence of bourgeois tendencies of thought. In the end, they were disheartened by the ineffectual struggle of intelligence against the mass mind, and in a spirit of resignation and sacrifice returned to their initial occupation, that of copyists.

The last part of the book was to be a compilation of the things that they copied, a record of human foolishness and unintelligent thought which is everywhere accepted as true and good because of the authority which it represents. During his life Flaubert had made a collection of sayings and ideas which are masterpieces of human stupidity on the part of both the experts and the common man. He hoped that the sight of all of these in a mass would make clear the inanity which may reside in authority.

[21]   *The Opposing Self* (New York, The Viking Press, 1955), p. 182.

The great interest in *L'Education sentimentale* and *Bouvard et Pécuchet* which has been manifested by American critics during the last thirty years can be accounted for by the importance that his meanings hold for modern readers. It has been pointed out that *Madame Bovary* benefited from the sociological implications that liberal critics found in the work. In the case of *Madame Bovary*, this interest took second place to esthetic criticism and the book's own long history as a classic. *L'Education sentimentale* was also utilized to demonstrate esthetic techniques of critical evaluation. But the book's greatest impact, along with that of *Bouvard et Pécuchet*, has been in the realm of ideas. The liberal critics have found in these two works of the last century a perfect expression of the intellectual trends and social attitudes which inhere in the twentieth century. Writers who are searching for a mode to express the needs of modern man bound in the restrictions of present-day materialism and ideology are becoming aware of these books as an important source for study.

Louise Bogan stressed the importance of Flaubert to modern American literature.[22] She wrote that Flaubert and Baudelaire are the fathers of modern literary creation. They charted a course for modern prose and poetry toward "innerness", poetic naturalism, the direct examination of the contemporary scene; toward the breaking of frames, mobility, plasticity, and inventiveness. Bouvard and Pécuchet represented for her the prototype of the modern individual. She claimed that Flaubert "gave the two simple-minded copyists a set of manias which is still complete for the dislocated middle-class mind of our time; manias ranging from the collecting of antiques to an absorption in various forms of science and politics. These two prototypes of the middle-class yearner with a few retouches could represent not only the modern lecture-listening audience, but many of the experts who tend the complicated machinery of modern civilization." [23]

Stratton Buck summed up this tendency in the modern liberal critic to find in Flaubert an oracle with the force to depict nakedly the condition of contemporary man.[24] He wrote that:

---

[22]   See Appendix A, 247.
[23]   *Selected Criticism* (New York, The Noonday Press, 1955), p. 8.
[24]   See Appendix A, 258.

It is possible that the man, Flaubert, is just as important to us, in this mid-twentieth century, as his work. We need his feeling of his own strength, of his ability to render, by force of unremitting labor, some portion of the vision that had been vouchsafed him. We need his awareness of the disparity between the life of the imagination and the life of reality, and his sense of the importance of the life of the imagination. We need the magnificent anger that fulminates through the letters, excoriating in splendid anathemas whatever is mean, vulgar, phony, pretentious, or self-seeking. We need his rare devotion to Beauty, his high conception of the artist's calling, the exacting standard, the integrity.

The most recent critical attitudes towards *L'Education sentimentale* and *Bouvard et Pécuchet* may help to explain the resurgence of interest in Flaubert that has been manifested in the United States in the last few years. The questions which these two books treat are those which modern man is asking himself. The problem of the conciliation of man's idealistic nature with a materialistic and ideological environment is the major theme of both of the works. And it is a theme which has preoccupied the attention of many contemporary readers.

VI

CONCLUSION

For nearly one hundred years the name of Flaubert has been an important one in American literary circles. From 1860, when the growing concern with realistic techniques was felt by American critics, until 1960, when esthetic evaluations and social problems dominate in literary studies, the novels of Flaubert have provided a rich source for study and inspiration. Two of his works, *Madame Bovary* and *Salammbô*, had a wide popular audience as well as ample critical attention before the turn of the century. *L'Education sentimentale* became the focus of diverse angles of observation in the mid-twentieth century. Because of his innovations and firm convictions concerning the art of creating fiction, their author became the center of discussion and the source of ideas during the crucial periods when American literary production was undergoing change and when American critical standards were being established.

Before 1900 two novels by Flaubert were well known in America. *Madame Bovary* had been published in English in 1881 and *Salammbô* in 1886. Both of the books were widely circulated here and had a wide popular reading audience. Both of them were the subject of critical articles. The early critical notices for the most part are characterized by two qualities. They were based almost completely upon stereotyped critical standards and showed an almost unanimous dependence upon the critic's personal prejudices.

From the sixties to the turn of the century the battle between realism and romanticism was waged. Flaubert had created the realistic techniques and incorporated all the technical elements of his art in *Madame Bovary*. This book became for modern writers a perfect model of the realistic novel. Flaubert based his realistic method upon the scientific observation of facts, selected and ordered in such a way as to achieve artistic unity. His subject matter was true to life drawn from the commonplace elements of society. The meaning of the book is to be found in its depiction of a member of society who attempts to establish a workable relationship with his environment. Every aspect of technique and subject matter had been carefully integrated in this novel for the purpose of creating a realistic portrayal of life consonant with the most rigid demands of style and artistic perfection.

For the American critics of the mid-nineteenth century, realism held no such meanings. They believed that the new techniques involved the mere collecting of details, usually about a distasteful subject in a mean setting, and the mechanical placement of all of the details on paper. In other words, they were not aware of the principle of artistic choice. The fact that an author of realistic works did not teach a moral but stood aside and let the facts speak for themselves was unacceptable to American critics before 1900. They felt that the composition of a realistic book was dull and depressing and that the moral picture presented was dangerous. Most American critics evaluated Flaubert's novel, *Madame Bovary*, on these grounds and found it lacking in the finer qualities. Only a few critics showed an impartial judgment regarding the novel, and these were ones usually predisposed to accept realistic methods. Howells defended *Madame Bovary* firmly on the grounds that it was moral, and that it demonstrated the power and effectiveness of realism in fiction. Henry James defended it on the basis of its esthetic values.

At the time that *Madame Bovary* appeared in English here, the battle for realism in the United States was approaching its climax. The book almost immediately became a best-seller. During the eighties the tone of criticism underwent a change. It was admitted that the book was moral and offered a strong lesson to young people concerning the wages of sin. Following the example of Henry James, the critics discussed Flaubert's techniques and found them to be useful and stimulating. His enormous artistry was highly praised. In the nineties, a decade before realism was accepted in the United States, *Madame Bovary* was firmly established as a masterpiece. Even those who still found it difficult to accept realism discovered other things in Flaubert's novel to recommend it. They concentrated upon the artistic

aspects of the work. They detected the presence of romantic tendencies which had not been obvious heretofore.

Salammbô, which appeared in English here in 1886, lent support to
the contention that Flaubert was really a romantic. His correspondence,
which had been published, and books about his life helped establish
this impression. For these reasons the critics believed that it was safe
for young writers to imitate Flaubert. They compared him with other
French writers and found a vast difference. Zola, whose novel, *Nana,*
had also been widely read in America, illustrated the difference between Flaubert and the writers who professed to be of his school. The
distinction was made between realism and naturalism. It was a common feeling that French writers after Flaubert had perverted his principles.

At the beginning of the twentieth century, realism had gained
acceptance in the United States. At the same time, schools of criticism
were developing here which maintained different standards and techniques. The neo-humanist, liberal, and esthetic schools of criticism
were all beginning to take definite form and to establish their own
criteria for excellence in the novel. By the turn of the century *Madame
Bovary* was held to be an indisputable classic, although the neo-
humanists found the novel lacking in high moral tone. In the early
years Flaubert's great preoccupation with art and form was severely
criticized because it was thought to lead to sterility of meaning and
content. An effort was made by some critics who appreciated Flaubert
to place him back among the romantics and thus reaffirm his respectability. All of the critics, however, recognized the enormous prestige
that he enjoyed in the novelistic field.

After the First World War a movement toward freedom of expression and experimentation manifested itself in the United States. *Madame Bovary* with its evident esthetic inspiration was available to the
young writers in this movement as a solid example of the validity of
their ideals. Esthetic criticism was one of the outgrowths of this manifestation; it did not depend upon Flaubert for its rise in America. The
sources of this school are varied and old. However, with the establishment of esthetic ideals as a major force in American criticism, *Madame
Bovary* has been the subject of intense study. Detailed analyses of
Flaubert's use of symbolism and his techniques of structure and form

by American critics have added greatly to the appreciation of his works. *Madame Bovary* is one of the earliest novels wherein may be found the conscious practice of esthetic principles as an integral part of a literary work.

Salammbô, La Tentation de Saint Antoine, and *Trois Contes* did not draw the wide and enduring critical attention in the United States that *Madame Bovary* did. Before the turn of the nineteenth century *Salammbô* enjoyed a fairly wide reading public but perhaps because this novel seemed romantic in tone, it did not elicit the controversial notices of its predecessor. *Trois Contes* received more favorable than bad notices here. This book, however, like *Salammbô* and *La Tentation,* has never been the center of much critical attention.

L'Eudcation sentimentale provided further study for the esthetic and liberal critics in the United States. Although it appeared in France before the *Tentation,* the novel has excited critical reaction here only within the last thirty years. It, too, has been judged as a marvelous example of the fusion of form and content which is a criterion of modern criticism. Its artistry is more striking than that of *Madame Bovary* because it is more extensive. Flaubert succeeded in doing in *L'Education* what Balzac tried to do in his series of novels which make up *La Comédie humaine.* In one novel Flaubert has compressed a whole period and depicted the essential spirit and essence of the life of that period. He perceived the controlling intellectual and philosophic impulse of the time and the effect which it was having upon the human spirit. With the greatest literary artistic workmanship he expressed the sentiment of modern man in the book. It is this element that American critics find so relevent today.

Until the esthetic and liberal critics began to study Flaubert's novels, the common opinion was that he was disinterested in social questions. Recently American critics have pointed out that *Madame Bovary* represented a quality of human nature that was inherent in everyone. They have enabled the reader to translate the setting of the novel from the limited background of Normandy to a more universal one. In *L'Education* this transformation is unnecessary. Modern criticism has clearly indicated the purpose which impelled Flaubert to write the novel and has shown his fervent concern for the problem of man and his modern environment.

Flaubert's books have been published in numerous editions in the United States and have been widely read. All of his major works have been translated into English for American consumption. *Madame Bovary*, in particular, has been translated many times by many translators. It still enjoys wide sales. Because of the great literary innovations inherent in this novel, succeeding generations of critics have sustained and furthered the interest which has attended it since its appearance.

Critical notices about Flaubert have varied greatly. He has always had strong advocates in the United States as well as many denigrators, but his first book maintained its high reputation in spite of adverse criticism. By 1900 his admirers almost constituted a cult, and this fact occasioned a reaction on the part of many who resented his attention to technique and art.

The critical consensus is that *Madame Bovary* is an important novel for seminal ideas of technique. Modern American concepts of realism conform to the pattern established by Flaubert in this novel. It has been reiterated by numerous critics that this book had an important pervasive influence on the modern novel in America as well as in Europe.

During the last twenty years *L'Education sentimentale* and *Bouvard et Pécuchet* have received increasing critical study in the United States. Because of the notices concerning these works, Flaubert has had a new dimension added to his reputation. His own ironic statements concerning the direction taken by the members of modern materialistic society have struck a responsive chord in recent critics who consider Flaubert as a source of inspiration. At the present time there are still those who admire Flaubert immensely and others who recognize his importance but dislike what he represents. As a stimulus to other writers, the effects of Flaubert's works are still being recorded and are apparent in contemporary American writing. And this stimulus is still being felt in ever-increasing measure by the modern critics of our American society.

APPENDIX A

PRIMARY SOURCES IN CHRONOLOGICAL ORDER

1. Anon., "Fiction as an Art", *Living Age*, XXXIX (1845), p. 356.
2. ——, "The French Novel", *Living Age*, XXXVII (1845), p. 99.
3. ——, "Current Literature", *Atlantic Monthly*, I (1857), p. 256.
4. ——, "The Lowest Deep in French Literature", *Living Age*, LXVII (1857), p. 451.
5. ——, "Literary Statistics for French for Fifteen Years", *Eclectic Magazne*, XIV (1858), p. 327.
6. ——, [No title], *Atlantic Monthly*, IX, (1862), p. 525.
7. ——, [No title], *Atlantic Monthly*, XI (1863), p. 239
8. ——, [No title], *Atlantic Monthly*, XVIII (1866), p. 768.
9. Arnold, M., "The Modern Element in Literature", *MacMillan's Magazine*, XIX (1867), p. 304.
10. Morris, W. P., "Gustave Flaubert, The Realist", *Lippincott's Monthly Magazine*, VI (1870), pp. 439-446.
11. James, H., [No title], *Atlantic Monthly*, XXX (1870), p. 251.
12. Anon., [No title], *Atlantic Monthly*, XXXI (1871), p. 249.
13. Howells, W. D., *A Chance Acquaintance* (Boston, 1873).
14. Potvin, C., Review of *De La Corruption littéraire en France*, in *Atlantic Monthly*, XXXII (1873), p. 734.
15. Ashton, P., "Modern French Fiction", *Lippincott's Monthly Magazine*, XIII (1874), pp. 237-244.
16. Anon, Review of *La Tentation de Saint Antoine*, in *Atlantic Monthly*, XXXIV (1874), p. 241.
17. Anon., [No title], *Atlantic Monthly*, XXXIV (1874), p. 745.
18. ——, "Realistic Techniques in the Novel", *Nation*, XVIII (1874), p. 364.
19. ——, [No title], *Atlantic Monthly*, XL (1877), p. 382.
20. Findlater, J. H. "Fiction, Is It Deteriorating", *Living Age*, CCXLI (1880), p. 134.
21. Anon., [No title], *Atlantic Monthly*, XLVI (1880), p. 697.
22. James, H., "A Note on Flaubert", *Atlantic Monthly*, L. (1882), p. 271.

23. Beard, R. O., "A Dangerous Tendency in the Novel", *Dial*, III (1883), p. 110.
24. Sedgewick, A. G., "The Novel of Today", *Nation*, XXXVI (1883), pp. 185-186.
25. Anon., "Realism and Reality", *The Harvard Monthly*, V (1883), p. 24.
26. James, H., "Ivan Turgenieff", *Atlantic Monthly*, LIII (1884), p. 53.
27. Norton, G., "Flaubert's Correspondence with Madame Sand", *Nation*, XXXVIII (1884), pp. 292-294.
28. Anon., "French Literature", *Atlantic Monthly*, LIII (1884), p. 857.
29. ——, "Novels", *Atlantic Monthly*, LIII (1884), p. 42; 727.
30. ——, [No title], *Atlantic Monthly*, LIII (1884), p. 112.
31. James, H., [No title], *Longman's Magazine*, IV (1884), p. 137.
32. ——, "Fiction in English and French", *MacMillan's Magazine*, L (1884), p. 250.
33. Norton, G., "The Art of Fiction", *Nation*, XXXIX (1884), pp. 260-261.
34. ——, "Recent Fiction", *Nation*, XXXVIII (1884), p. 292.
35. ——, "George Sand and Gustave Flaubert", *Nation*, XXXIX (1884), pp. 337-338.
36. Lee, V., "A Dialogue on Novels", *Living Age*, CLXVII (1885), pp. 233-246.
37. Stillman, W. J., "Realism and Idealism", *Nation*, XLI (1885), p. 545; XLII (1886), p. 107.
38. Norton, G., "The Shorter Pieces of Flaubert", *Nation*, XLII (1886), pp. 107-108.
39. ——, Review of *Salambô*, in *Critic*, V (1886), p. 243.
40. Anon., [No title], *Dial*, VIII (1886), p. 277.
41. ——, Review of *Salambô*, in *The Literary World*, XVII (1886), p. 481.
42. Adam, J., "French Novels — Real to Life?", *North American Review*, CLIII (1887), p. 536.
43. Anon., Review of *Trois Contes*, in *Atlantic Monthly*, LX (1887), p. 382.
44. ——, [No title], *Harper's Magazine*, LXXV (1887), p. 155.
45. Laugel, A., "Flaubert's Correspondence", *Nation*, XLIV (1887), pp. 385-386.
46. Saltus, E., "The Future of Fiction", *North Amercan Review*, CXLIX (1889), p. 580.
47. Fletcher, J. B., " 'Madame Bovary' ", *Harvard Monthly*, X (1888), p. 14; 79.
48. Hooper, L. H., "The Modern French Novel", *Lippincott's Monthly Magazine*, XX (1888), p. 379.
49. Norton, G., "Recent Fiction", *Nation*, XLVI (1888), p. 529.
50. Eggleston, E., "Modern Fiction", *Forum*, III (1890), p. 286.

51. Gosse, E., "The Limits of Realism in Fiction", *Forum*, V (1890), p. 391.
52. Venner, A., "French Literature", *Lippincott's Monthly Magazine*, XXII (1890), p. 335.
53. Roe, E. P., "The Element of Life in Fiction", *Forum*, V (1891), p. 226.
54. Thompson, A., "Realism in Fiction", *Critic*, IX (1891), p. 19.
55. Anon., "Two French Men of Letters", *Atlantic Monthly*, LXVIII (1891), p. 695.
56. ——, "Contrasts of French Literature and English Literature", *MacMillan's Magazine*, LXIII (1891), p. 330.
57. James, H., "Gustave Flaubert", *MacMillan's Magazine*, LXVII (1892), pp. 332-343.
58. Hale, E. E., "Some Further Aspects of Realism", *Dial*, XIV (1893), pp. 169-171.
59. James, H., *Essays in London* (London, 1893).
60. Lewin, W., "The Abuse of Fiction", *Forum*, VII (1893), p. 659.
61. Rollins, A. W., "Reality and Realism", *Critic*, XI (1893), p. 123.
62. Stanley, H., "Passion for Realism", *Dial*, XIV (1894), p. 238.
63. Cutting, M. D., "Two Forces in Fiction", *Forum*, X (1895), p. 216.
64. Hannigan, D. F., "Book Reviews", *Westminster Review*, CXLIV (1895), pp. 385-392.
65. Hyde, G. M., "The Allotrophy of Realism", *Dial*, XVIII (1895), pp. 231-232.
66. Lang, A., "Tendencies in Fiction", *North American Review*, CLXI (1895), p. 153.
67. Peck, H. T., Review of J. C. Tarver's *Gustave Flaubert*, in *Bookman*, II (1895), pp. 130-133.
68. Smith, I., Review of Tarver's *Gustave Flaubert*, in *Dial*, XIX (1895), pp. 208-210.
69. Sully, E., "The Future of Fiction", *Forum*, IX (1895), p. 644.
70. Tarver, J. C., *Gustave Flaubert as Seen in his Works and Correspondence* (New York, 1895).
71. Anon., Review of J. C. Tarver's *Gustave Flaubert*, in *Critic*, XXVII (1895), p. 245.
72. Newman, E., "Book Reviews", *Fortnightly Review*, LXIV (1895), p. 813.
73. Anon., "The New Fiction", *Living Age*, CLIV (1895), p. 688.
74. Barr, A. E., "The Modern Novel", *North American Review*, CLIX (1896), p. 285.
75. Logan, A. M., "The Study of the Novel", *Nation*, LXIII (1896), p. 264.
76. Anon., "Moral Elements in Literature", *Living Age*, CXLVII (1896), p. 545.

77. ——, "Novelists and the Novel", *Living Age*, CLXX (1896), p. 358.
78. ——, "Growth of the American Novel", *Living Age*, CLXX (1896), p. 771.
79. ——, "Contemporary Fiction", *Living Age*, CLXXII (1896), p. 771.
80. ——, "Gustave Flaubert", *Scribner's Magazine*, XIX (1896), p. 391.
81. Anderson, M. S., "A New Ideal in Fiction", *Dial*, XXIII (1897), pp. 269-270.
82. Blakeman, W. C., "A Century of American Fiction", *Dial*, XXV (1898), pp. 9-11.
83. Crawford, F. M., "What is a Novel?", *Forum*, XIV (1898), p. 591.
84. Howells, W. D., "The New Fiction", *North American Review*, CLXXI (1900), p. 935.
85. ——, "A Psychological Countercurrent in Fiction", *North American Review*, CLXXIII (1901), p. 872.
86. Anon., "Fiction Made Easy", *MacMillan's Magazine*, LXXXIV (1901), p. 31.
87. MacLaren, D., Review of *Salammbô*, in *Bookman*, XIV (1901), p. 193.
88. Boyeson, H. H., "Great Realists and Empty Story Tellers", *Forum*, XVIII (1903), p. 724.
89. Anon., "The Style of Gustave Flaubert", *Bookman*, XVI (1903), pp. 529-531.
90. Marzials, F. T., "Gustave Flaubert", *Critic*, XLIII (1903), pp. 148-152.
91. Edwards, A. B., "The Art of the Novelist", *Living Age*, CCII (1904), p. 771.
92. Huneker, J. G., *Overtones* (New York, 1904).
93. Lang, A., "The Purpose of the Novel", *Critic*, XXII (1904), p. 30.
94. Moffat, W. D., "Plea for the Novel", *Critic*, XXII (1904), p. 230.
95. Anon., "The Irresponsible Novelist", *Living Age*, CCV (1904), p. 774.
96. Cobbe, F. P., "Morals of Literature", *Eclectic Magazin*, LXIII (1907), p. 72.
97. Deshays, E., "Genesis of a Masterpiece", *Bookman*, XXVI (1907), p. 420.
98. Johnson, C., and Ch. Gosse, "Flaubert's Letters", *North American Review*, CLXXXV (1907), pp. 437-441.
99. Bailey, P., "Gustave Flaubert, A Psychological Study", *Bookman*, XX (1908), pp. 212-221.
100. Anon., "The Decline in French Influence", *Living Age*, CCXXXIV (1908), p. 58.
101. James, W. P., "A Martyr for Style", *Living Age*, CCLXI (1909), pp. 570-573.

102. Fitzgerald, E., "The Spirit of Flaubert", *Putnam's Magazine*, VII (1910), p. 572.
103. Coleman, A., "The Influence of English Literature on Flaubert before 1851", *MLN*, 1911, p. 143.
104. Anon., "Flaubert's Opinions", *Bookman*, XXXIV (1911), pp. 132-133.
105. Coleman, A., "Some Inconsistencies in 'Salammbô', in *MLN*, XXVII (1912), p. 123.
106. Anon., "The Novel, Will It Disappear?", *North American Review*, CLXXV (1912), p. 289.
107. Blossom, F., Review of Descharmes' *Autour de Flaubert*, in *MLN*, XXVIII (1913), p. 180.
108. Goddard, A., "Fiction for the People", *Lippincott's Monthly Magazine*, XLV (1913), p. 875.
109. Repplier, A., "Reality in Fiction", *Lippincott's Monthly Magazine*, XLV (1913), p. 908.
110. Coleman, A., "Recent Flaubert Literature", *MLN*, XXIX (1914), p. 181.
111. Faguet, E., *Gustave Flaubert* (Boston, 1914).
112. Fay, P. B., and A. Coleman, *Sources and Structure of Flaubert's "Salammbô"* (Baltimore, 1914).
113. James, H., *Notes on Novelists* (New York, 1914).
114. Showerman, G., "Balzac and Flaubert", *Dial*, LVII (1914), p. 502.
115. Armstrong, E. C., ed., *Elliott Monographs in the Romance Languages and Literatures* (Princeton, N.J., 1915).
116. Colby, F. M., "The Book of the Month", *North American Review*, CCI (1915), pp. 273-276.
117. Coleman, A., *Flaubert's Literary Development in the Light of his "Mémoires d'un fou", "Novembre", and "Education sentimentale"* (Baltimore, 1915).
118. Parker, G., "The Art of Fiction", *Critic*, XXXIII (1915), p. 467.
119. Shanks, L. P., "The Romanticism of Flaubert", *Dial*, LIX (1915), pp. 316-318.
120. Buzlar, F. C., "Realism in Fiction", *Lippincott's Monthly Magazine*, XLVIII (1916), p. 94.
121. Hubbard, A. P., "A Note on Flaubert's Novels", *MLN*, XXXI (1916), p. 405.
122. Anon., "Modern French Literature", *Eclectic Magazine*, LXXII (1916), p. 534.
123. Wright, W. H., "Flaubert, A Re-evaluation", *North American Review*, CCVI (1917), pp. 455-463.
124. Hamilton, A., *Sources of the Religious Element in Flaubert's "Salammbô"* (Baltimore, 1918).
125. Flower, B. O., "Fashions in Fiction", *Arena*, XXX (1919), p. 287.

126. Pater, W., *Sketches and Reviews* (New York, 1919).
127. Anon., "Gustave Flaubert", *Living Age*, CCC (1919), pp. 496-498.
128. Harris, F., *Latest Contemporary Portraits* (New York, 1920).
129. Riddell, A. R., *Flaubert and Maupassant: A Literary Relationship* (Chicago, 1920).
130. Bowen, R., Review of *Flaubert and Maupassant: A literary Relationship*, in *MLN*, XXXVI (1921), p. 293.
131. Boyd, E., "Gustave Flaubert, A Retrospect (Dec. 1821-Dec. 1921)", *The Independent*, CVII (1921), pp. 340-341.
132. Cowley, M., "Literary Review: This Younger Generation", *New York Evening Post*, Oct. 15, 1921.
133. Huneker, J. G., *Egoists* (New York, 1921).
134. Pound, E., *Polite Essays* (Norfolk, Conn. 1921).
135. Schiefley, W. H., "The Centenary of Flaubert", *North American Review*, CCXIV (1921), pp. 809-816.
136. Anon., "Gustave Flaubert: 1821-1921", *Nation*, CXIII (1921), pp. 33-34.
137. ——, [No title], *New Republic*, XXVII (1921), p. 10.
138. Burke, K., "The Correspondence of Flaubert", *Dial*, LXXII (1922), pp. 145-155.
139. Carrière, J., *Degeneration in the Great French Masters* (New York, 1922).
140. Pound, E., "Paris Letter", *Dial*, LXXIII (1922), pp. 332-337.
141. Woodbridge, M., "Flaubert and War Brides", *MLN*, XXXVII (1922), pp. 183-185.
142. Anon., "Re-estimating the Patron Saint of Modern Realistic Fiction", *Current Opinion*, LXXII (1922), pp. 382-385.
143. Murry, J. M., "Flaubert's Literary Limits", *Living Age*, CCCXII (1922), pp. 227-234.
144. Brandeis, G., *Creative Spirits* (New York, 1923).
145. Hearn, L., *Essays in European and Oriental Literature* (New York, 1923).
146. Bradford, G., "Bare Souls", *Harper's Magazine*, CXLIX (1924), pp. 373-384.
147. David, H. C., *Flaubert and Georges Sand in their Correspondence* (Chicago, 1924).
148. Murry, J. M., "Flaubert and Flaubart", *Yale Review*, XIII (1924), p. 347.
149. Sherman, S. P., *Points of View* (New York, 1924).
150. Anon., "Decay of the Novel", *Critic*, XLII (1924), p. 59.
151. Coleman, A., "Some Sources of Flaubert's 'Smarh'", *MLN*, XL (1925), p. 205.
152. Dillingham, L. B., "Source of 'Salammbô'", *MLN*, XL (1925), p. 71.

153. Frierson, W. C., "The Naturalistic Techniques of Flaubert", *French Quarterly*, VII (1925), p. 178.
154. Fuller, E., "Decadent Novel", *Lippincott's Monthly Magazine*, LVII (1925), p. 427.
    (1925), p. 1.
155. Henderson, A., "Aspects of Contemporary Fiction", *Arena*, XXXVI
156. Patzer, O., "Unwritten Works of Flaubert", *MLN*, XLI (1926), p. 24.
157. Hearn, L., *Life and Literature* (New York, 1927).
158. Lewisohn, L., *Cities and Men* (New York, 1927).
159. Maurice, A. B., "A Note and a Difficulty", *Bookman,* LXVI (1927), pp. 275-276.
160. Rascoe, B., "Le Mot juste", *Bookman*, LXVI (1927), p. 275.
161. Shanks, L. P., *Flaubert's Youth, 1821-1845* (Baltimore, 1927).
162. Zola, E., *Les Romanciers naturalistes* (Paris, 1928).
163. Anon., "A Note on Flaubert", *Bookman,* LXVII (1928), pp. 409-410.
164. Jackson, J., "A Note on Flaubert", *MLN*, XLIV (1929), p. 538.
165. Anon., "Letters to Turgenev", *Living Age*, CCCXXXVII (1929), pp. 295-300.
166. James, H., *The Art of Fiction* (London, 1930).
167. Anon., "A Flaubert Love Letter", *Living Age*, CCCXXXVIII (1930), p. 96.
168. Durant, W., *Adventures in Genius* (New York, 1931).
169. Wilson, E., *Axel's Castle* (New York, 1931).
170. Canu, J., "Flaubert et la phrase finale d'*Une Vie*", *MLN*, XLVII (1932), p. 26.
171. Rascoe, B., *Titans of Literature* (New York, 1932).
172. Anon., "Flaubert's Note Book", *Living Age,* CCCXLI (1932), p. 461.
173. Canu, J., "La Couleur normande de 'Madame Bovary' ", *PMLA*, XLVIII (1933), p. 167.
174. Jasper, G., "Saint Antoine", *MLN*, XLVIII (1933), p. 162.
175. Melcher, E., "Flaubert et Henri Monnier: A Study of the Bourgeois", *MLN*, XLVIII (1933), p. 156.
176. Ferguson, W. D., *The Influence of Flaubert on George Moore* (Philadelphia, 1934).
177. Thibaudet, A., "Flaubert in Love", *Living Age*, CCCXLVI (1934), pp. 456-457.
178. Lewis, W., *Men Without Art* (London, 1934).
179. Maugham, S., *Flaubert and Madame Bovary* (New York, 1934).
180. Miller, L., "Gustave Flaubert and Charles Baudelaire", *PMLA*, XLIX (1934), p. 630.
181. Denoeu, F., "L'ombre de 'Madame Bovary' ", *PMLA*, L (1935), p. 1165.

182. Cather, W., *Not Under Forty* (New York, 1936).
183. Colum, M., "Literature of Today and Tomorrow", *Scribner's Magazine*, C (1936), p. 66.
184. Alden, D. W., "Proust and the Flaubert Controversy", *Romanic Review*, XXVIII (1937), pp. 230-240.
185. Colum, M., *From These Roots* (New York, 1937).
186. Jackson, J., *Louise Colet et ses amis littéraires* (New Haven, 1937).
187. ——, "Flaubert's Correspondence with Louise Colet", *Romanic Review*, XXVIII (1937), p. 346.
188. Loveman, A., "Clearing House", *Romanic Review*, XVI (1937), p. 19.
189. Muller, H., *Modern Fiction* (New York, 1937).
190. Weinberg, B., *French Realism: The Critical Reaction* (PMLA, 1937).
191. Wilson, E., *The Triple Thinkers* (New York, 1938).
192. David, S., "Carol Kennicott de Main Street et sa lignée europeénne", *Revue de la Littérature Comparée*, XIX (1939), pp. 407-416.
193. Frienmuth, E. von H., *German Criticism of Gustave Flaubert, 1857-1930* (New York, 1939).
194. Jackson, J., "Madame Bovary, c'est moi", *Romanic Review*, XIX (1939), p. 11.
195. Steegmuller, F., *Flaubert and "Madame Bovary"* (New York, 1939).
196. ——, "Madam Bovary on Trial", *Romanic Review*, XIX (1939), p. 13.
197. Finch, G., "Comic Sense of Flaubert in the Light of Bergson's 'Le Rire' ", *PMLA*, LV (1940), p. 511.
198. Singer, A. E., "Flaubert's 'Une Nuit de Don Juan' ", *MLN*, LV (1940), p. 516.
199. Blackmur, R., "Humanism and Symbolic Imagination", *Southern Review*, VII (1941), p. 309.
200. Bruneau, J., "Flaubert's Influence on Henry James", *American Literature*, XIII (1941), pp. 240-256.
201. Bogan, L., "Sentimental Education Today", *Nation*, CLV (1942), pp. 301-302.
202. Seznec, J., "Science et Religion chez Flaubert", *Romanic Review*, XXXIII (1942), pp. 360-365.
203. Brown, D. F., "The Veil of Tanit", *Romanic Review*, XXXIV (1943), pp. 196-210.
204. Seznec, J., "Saint Antoine et les monstres", *PMLA*, LVIII (1943), p. 195.
205. Tate, A., "Techniques of Fiction", *Sewanee Review*, LII (1944), pp. 210-225.
206. ——, "Gustave Flaubert", *Magazine of the Légion d'Honneur*, XV (1944), pp. 265-278.
207. Seznec, J., "Flaubert, historien des hérésies dans la 'Tentation' ",

Romanic Review, XXXVI (1945), pp. 200; 314.

208. ——, "Notes on Flaubert and the United States", Magazine of the Légion d'Honneur, XVII (1946), pp. 391-398.

209. Aldridge, J., "The New Generation of Writers", Harper's Magazine, CXCV (1947), pp. 423-432.

210. Bart, B. F., "The Moral of Flaubert's Saint Julien", Romanic Review, XXXVIII (1947), p. 23.

211. Bonwitt, M., "Significance of the Dog in Flaubert's 'Education sentimentale'", PMLA, LXII (1947), p. 517.

212. Maugham, S., "Ten Best Novels", Atlantic Monthly, CLXXX (1947), p. 134.

213. Adams, R., "Masks and Delays", Sewanee Review, LVI (1948), p. 272.

214. Gordon, C., "Notes on Faulkner and Flaubert", Hudson Review, VI (1948), p. 222.

215. Levin, H., "Flaubert and the Spirit of '48", Yale Review, XXXVIII (1948), p. 96.

216. ——, "Portrait of an Artist as a Saint", Kenyon Review, X (1948), pp. 28-43.

217. Engstrom, A. G., "Flaubert's Correspondence and the Ironic and Symbolic Structure of 'Madame Bovary'", Studies in Philology, XLVI (1949), pp. 470-495.

218. Stallman, R. W., Critiques and Essays in Criticism 1920-1948, (New York, 1949).

219. Engstrom, A. G., "Dante, Flaubert and the 'Snows of Kilimanjaro'", MLN, LXV (1950), p. 203.

220. Bogan, L., "Modernism in American Literature", The American Quarterly, II (1950), p. 99.

221. Bonwitt, M., Flaubert et le principe de l'impassibilité (Berkeley, Calif., 1950).

222. Iglesias, A., "Classic Blend in Literature, 'Madame Bovary'", Romanic Review, XXXIII (1950), p. 7.

223. Van Ghent, D., "Clarissa and Emma as Phèdre", Partisan Review, XVII (1950), p. 820.

224. Auerbach, E., "In the Hôtel de la Mole", Partisan Review, XVIII (1951), p. 265.

225. Bart, B. F., "Balzac and Flaubert: Energy Versus Art", Romanic Review, XLII (1951), p. 198.

226. Blackmur, R., "Beauty out of Place", Kenyon Review, XIII (1951), pp. 475-503.

227. ——, The Portable Henry James (New York, 1951).

228. Orrock, D. H., "Hemingway, Hugo, and Revelation", MLN, LXVI (1951), p. 441.

229. Turnell, M., The Novel in France (New York, 1951).

230. Brooks, V. W., "Faith Versus Doubt in Literature", *Romanic Review*, XXXV (1952), p. 12.
231. Buck, S., "Chronology of the 'Education sentimentale'", *MLN*, LXVII (1952), p. 86.
232. Burke, K., *Counterstatement* (Los Altos, Calif., 1952).
233. Frohock, W. N., "Energy Versus Art—A Suggested Alternative", *Romanic Review*, XLIII (1952), p. 155.
234. Spencer, P., *Flaubert* (London, 1952).
235. Rossi, L., "The Structure of Flaubert's 'Bouvard et Pécuchet'", *Modern Language Quarterly*, XIV (1953), pp. 102-111.
236. Spitzer, L., "Balzac and Flaubert Again", *MLN*, LXVIII (1953), p. 583.
237. Steegmuller, F., "Love, Happiness, and Art", *Partisan Review*, XX (1953), p. 86.
238. Clemens, P., "D'un Mot mis en sa place", *Romanic Review*, XLV (1954), pp. 45-54.
239. Edel, L., "The Two Flauberts", *Nation*, CLXXVIII (1954), pp. 361-362.
240. Goodman, P., *The Structure of Literature* (Chicago, 1954).
241. Bart, B. F., "Esthetic Distance in 'Madam Bovary'", *PMLA*, LXIX (1954), p. 1112.
242. Grubbs, H., "Fictional Time and Chronology in 'Education sentimentale'", *Kentucky Foreign Language Quarterly*, IV (1954), p. 183.
243. Kazin, A., "The Anger of Flaubert", *New Yorker*, XXX (1954), pp. 145-151.
244. Shattuck, R., "Priest of Style", *Romanic Review*, XXXVII (1954), p. 23.
245. Spencer, P., "Flaubert's Enigma", *New Republic*, CXXX (1954), p. 17.
246. Anon., "French Mutt and Jeff", *Time Magazine*, LXIII (1954), pp. 120-122.
247. Bogan, L., *Selected Criticism* (New York, 1955).
248. Poulet, G., "The Circle and the Center", *Western Review*, XIX (1955), pp. 245-260.
249. Tindall, W. Y., *The Literary Symbol* (New York, 1955).
250. Trilling, L., *The Opposing Self* (New York, 1955).
251. Untermeyer, L., *Makers of the Modern World* (New York, 1955).
252. Dauner, L., "Poetic Symbolism in 'Madame Bovary'", *South Atlantic Quarterly*, LV (1956), p. 207.
253. Gibian, G., "Love by the Book; Pushkin, Stendhal, Flaubert", *Comparative Literature*, VIII (1956), pp. 97-109.
254. Grenier, C., "The Art of Fiction: An Interview with William Faulkner", *Accent*, XVI (1956), p.p. 167-171.

255. Lapp, J. C., "Art and Hallucination in Flaubert", *French Studies,* X (1956), pp. 322-334.
256. Bart, B. F., *Flaubert's Landscape Descriptions* (Ann Arbor, Mich., 1957).
257. Bédé, J. A., "Jules de Gautier et Bovarisme", *Magazine of the Légion d'Honneur,* XXVIII (1957), pp. 9-36.
258. Buck, S., "For Emma Bovary", *Sewanee Review,* LXV (1957), pp. 551-564.
259. Fellows, O., "The Anniversary Translation of a French Classic, 'Madame Bovary'", *Romanic Review,* XL (1957), p. 21.
260. Giraud, R. D., *The Unheroic Hero in the Novels of Stendhal, Balzac and Flaubert* (New Brunswick, N. J., 1957).
261. Gordon, C., *How to Read a Novel* (New York, 1957).
262. Hatzfeld, H., "Les Contributions importantes à l'élucidation de l'art du 'Fleurs du mal' et 'Madame Bovary'", *Orbis Litterarum,* XII (1957), pp. 244-254.
263. Mercier, V., "Limitations of Flaubert", *Kenyon Review,* XIX (1957), p. 400.
264. Nelson, R. J., "'Madame Bovary' as Tragedy", *Modern Language Quarterly,* XVIII (1957), pp. 323-330.
265. Spiller, R., *The Cycle of American Literature* (New York, 1957).
266. Thorlby, A., *Gustave Flaubert and the Art of Realism* (New Haven, Conn., 1957).
267. Turnell, M., "Madame Bovary", *Sewanee Review,* LXV (1957), pp. 530-550.
268. Sachs, M., "Review", *Romanic Review,* XLVIII (1957), p. 19.
269. Anon., "Centenary of 'Madame Bovary'", *Saturday Review,* XL (1957), p. 21.
270. Arnold, A., "Why Structure in Fiction: A note to Social Scientists", *American Quarterly,* X (1958), pp. 325-330.
271. Bart, B. F., "'Madame Bovary' after a Century", *French Review,* XXXI (1958), p. 203.
272. ——, "Virgil, Ovid and the Cry of Fate in 'Madame Bovary'", *Philological Quarterly,* XXXVII (1958), p. 123.
273. Madsen, B. G., "Realism, Irony, and Compassion in Flaubert's 'Un Cœur simple'", *French Review,* XXVII (1958), pp. 253-258.
274. Hemmings, F. W., "Zola and 'L'Education sentimentale'", *Romanic Review,* L (1959), p. 35.
275. Kazin, A., *The Inmost Leaf* (New York, 1959).

CHRONOLOGICAL LIST OF FLAUBERT'S WORKS DISTRIBUTED IN ENGLISH IN THE UNITED STATES

1881: *Madame Bovary*, trans. John Stirling (pseud.), (Philadelphia, T. B. Peterson and Bros).

1885: *Salammbô*, trans. M. French Sheldon (New York, Lovell, Coryell and Co.).

1886: *Salammbô*, trans. M. French Sheldon, 3 eds. (New York, Saxon and Co.).

1891: *Madame Bovary*, trans. John Stirling (pseud.), 2 eds. (Philadelphia, T. B. Peterson and Bros).

Madame Bovary, or *Loved to the Last*, trans. Eleanor Marx-Aveling (Chicago, Laird and Lee).

Salammbô, trans. J. S. Chartres (Chicago, Charles H. Sergel and Co.).

1892: *Salammbô*, trans. M. French Sheldon (New York, Lovell, Coryell and Co.)

1896: *Madame Bovary* (subscribers only), (Philadelphia, G. Barrie and Son).

1900: *Salammbô*, trans. Zenaide A. Ragozin (New York, G. Putnam's Sons).

1901: *Madame Bovary, Provincial Manners*, trans. Eleanor Marx-Aveling (New York, G. Munro's Sons).

1902: *Madame Bovary,* trans. W. Blaydes, introd. by Henry James (New York, D. Appleton and Co.).

1903: *Gustave Flaubert, Little French Masterpieces*, trans. G. E. Ives (New York, G. Putnam's Sons).

1904: *The Complete Works of Gustave Flaubert* (subscribers only) (New York, M. W. Dunne).

1905: *Madame Bovary* (Connoisseur edition) (New York, Société des Beaux Arts).

Madame Bovary, trans. W. Walton (Chicago, Laird and Lee).

The Legend of Saint Julian, Hospitaler, trans. Agnes Lee (Portland, Maine, T. B. Mosher).

1906: *Salammbô*, trans. Zenaide A. Ragozin (New York, G. Putnam's Sons).

1909: *Gustave Flaubert, Little French Masterpieces,* trans. G. B. Ives (New York, G. Putnam's Sons).

1910: *Stories,* trans. F. White (New York, Dutton).

The Temptation of Saint Anthony, trans. Lafcadio Hearn (New York, Alice Hariman Co.).

1911: *The Temptation of Saint Anthony,* trans. Lafcadio Hearn (New York, Alice Hariman Co.).

1915: *The First Temptation of Saint Anthony,* trans. René Francis (New York, Brentano's).

1918: *Madame Bovary,* trans. Eleanor Marx-Aveling (New York, Boni Liveright, Inc.).

1919: *Madame Bovary,* trans. Eleanor Marx-Aveling (New York, A. Knopf).

Madame Bovary, trans. Dora K. Ranous (New York, Brentano's).

Salammbô, trans. Dora K. Ranous (New York, Brentano's).

1920: *The Temptation of Saint Anthony,* trans. Lafcadio Hearn (New York, Boni Liveright).

1921: *Georges Sand and Gustave Flaubert Letters,* trans. Aimee L. McKenzie (New York, Boni Liveright).

1922: *A Sentimental Education,* trans. Dora K. Ranous (New York, Brentano's).

1923: *Flaubert's Complete Works,* 10 vols. (New York, M. H. Wise and Co.).

The Temptation of Saint Anthony and The Legend of Saint Julian the Hospitaler, trans. Dora K. Ranous (New York, Brentano's).

1924: *Three Tales,* trans. Arthur MacDowell (New York, A. Knopf).

1927: *Flaubert's Works,* 10 vols. (New York, Dingwell Rock).

Salammbô, trans. Ben R. Redman (New York, John Day, Co.).

Gustave Flaubert, Little French Masterpices, trans. G. B. Ives (New York, G. Putnam's Sons).

Herodias, 2 eds. (New York, G. Putnam's Sons).

1928: *Madame Bovary,* trans. J. L. May (New York, Dodd Mead and Co).

Madame Bovary, trans. Eleanor Marx-Aveling (New York, E. P. Dutton and Co.).

Golden Tales from Flaubert (New York, Dodd Mead and Co.).

1929: *Salammbô,* trans. Dora K. Ranous (New York, Modern Library).

Bibliomania, trans. T. W. Koch (Evanston, Ill., Northwestern University Library).

1930: *Madame Bovary* (New York, Charles Scribner's Sons).

Madame Bovary, trans. Dora K. Ranous (New Yorks, Boni Liveright).

Madame Bovary, trans. Eleanor Marx-Aveling (New York, P. Smith).

Salammbô, trans. Dora K. Ranous (New York, Boni Liveright).

Salammbô (New York, Brown House).

Salammbô, trans. J. W. Mathews (New York, Mandrake Press).

The Legend of Saint Julian the Hospitaler, trans. M. D. Honey (New York, McKay).

The Temptation of Saint Anthony, trans. Lafcadio Hearn (New York, I. Washburn).

The Temptation of Saint Anthony, trans. Lafcadio Hearn (New York, Williams, Belasco and Meyers).

1931: *Madame Bovary*, trans. Eleanor Marx-Aveling (New York, Grosset and Dunlap).

Madame Bovary, trans. Henry Beauchamp (New York, Collins Press).

Salammbô, trans. E. Powers Mathers, 2 eds. (Waltham, Mass., Golden Cockerel Press).

Salammbô, trans. J. S. Chartres (New York, E. P. Dutton Co.).

Salammbô, trans. J. S. Chartres, 3 ed., enlarged (New York, E. P. Dutton Co.).

Salammbô, trans. E. Powers Mathers (New York, Random House).

1932: *Madame Bovary*, trans. Eleanor Marx-Aveling (New York, Florin Books).

Madame Bovary, trans. F. Jellinek (New York, Roman Press).

Madame Bovary, trans. Eleanor Marx-Aveling (Toronto, Nelson).

Madame Bovary, trans. Eleanor Marx-Aveling (New York, Godwin Press).

The Temptation of Saint Anthony, trans. Lafcadio Hearn (New York, Harper and Bros).

Salammbô (New York, Godwin Press).

November, trans. F. Jellinek (New York, Roman Press).

1933: *Best Known Works of Flaubert* (New York, Harper and Bros).

Selected Works of Flaubert (Toronto, Black).

Best Known Works of Gustave Flaubert (Toronto, Blue Ribbon Books Inc.).

1934: *Madame Bovary* (New York, E. P. Dutton Co.).

1935: *Salammbô* (Washington, D. C., The National Home Library Foundation).

Two Tales of Flaubert, trans. J. Combs (New York, MacMillan Co.).

1938: *Madame Bovary*, trans. Eleanor Marx-Aveling (New York, Limited Editions Club).

1941: *Madame Bovary*, trans. Eleanor Marx-Aveling (New York, Grosset and Dunlap).

Sentimental Education (New York, E. P. Dutton Co.).

1942: *Best Known Works of Gustave Flaubert*, 3 eds. (Toronto, Blue Ribbon Books).

1943: *The Temptation of Saint Anthony*, trans. Lafcadio Hearn (New York, Limited Editions Club).

1944: *Madame Bovary*, trans. Gerard M. Hopkins (New York, Peter Pauper Press).

Three Tales, trans. Arthur MacDowell (Norfolk, Conn., New Directions).

1948: *Madame Bovary* (New York, Rinehart).

Madame Bovary, trans. Eleanor Marx-Aveling (New York, Mc-Clelland).

Madame Bovary, trans. Eleanor Marx-Aveling (Cleveland, World Publishing Co.).

1949: *Madame Bovary*, trans. Gerard M. Hopkins (New York, Oxford University Press).

Madame Bovary, trans. Joan Charles (Philadelphia, J. C. Winston Co.).

1950: *Madame Bovary*, trans. Eleanor Marx-Aveling (New York, Pocket Books).

Madame Bovary, trans. Eleanor Marx-Aveling (New York, Harper and Bros.).

Madame Bovary, trans. Eleanor Marx-Aveling (New York, Modern Library).

Madame Bovary, trans. J. L. May (New York, Limited Editions Club).

Madame Bovary, trans. J. L. May (New York, Heritage Press).

The Temptation of Saint Anthony, trans. Lafcadio Hearn (Garden City, N.Y., Halcyon Press).

1954: *Bouvard and Pécuchet*, trans. T. W. Earp and G. W. Stonier (Norfolk, Conn., New Directions).

A Dictionary of Accepted Ideas, trans. Jacques Barzun (Norfolk, Conn., New Directions).

A Dictionary of Platitudes, trans. E. J. Gluck (Emmaus, Pa., Rodale Books).

Selected Letters of Gustave Flaubert, trans. F. Steegmuller, 2 eds. (New York, Farrar and Strauss).

1956: *Salammbô*, trans. J. S. Chartres (New York, E. P. Dutton Co.).

1957: *Madame Bovary*, trans. F. Steegmuller (New York, Random House).

Madame Bovary, trans. F. Steegmuller (New York, Modern Library).

A Sentimental Education, trans. Anthony Goldsmith (New York, E. P. Dutton Co.).

Selected Letters of Gustave Flaubert, trans. F. Steegmuller (New

York, Vintage Press).

1958: *A Sentimental Education* (Norfolk, Conn. New Directions).

1959: *Madame Bovary*, trans. Gerard M. Hopkins (New York, Oxford University Press).

APPENDIX C

LIST OF PH. D. DISSERTATIONS ABOUT FLAUBERT SUBMITTED TO AMERICAN UNIVERSITIES

1914: Blossom, F. A., "La Composition de 'Salammbô' d'après la correspondance de Flaubert (1857-1862)" (Baltimore, Johns Hopkins University).

1915: Coleman, Algernon, "Flaubert's Literary Development in the Light of his 'Mémoires d'un fou', 'Novembre' and 'Education sentimentale,'" (Baltimore, Johns Hopkins University).

1918: Hamilton, Arthur, "Sources of the Religious Element in Flaubert's 'Salammbô'" (Baltimore, Johns Hopkins University).

1934: Ferguson, W. D., "The Influence of Flaubert on George Moore" (Philadelphia, University of Pennsylvania).

1936: Presta, P. S., "The Social Attitude of the French Realists: a Study of Flaubert, the Goncourt Brothers, Maupassant and Alphonse Daudet" (Urbana, University of Illinois).

1937: Carter, B. G., "The French Realists and the Theatre: Gustave Flaubert, the Goncourt Brothers and Alphonse Daudet" (Urbana, University of Illinois).

1937: Weinberg, Bernard, "French Realism: the Critical Reaction, 1830-1870" (Chicago, University of Chicago).

1942: Buck, Stratton, "The 'Education sentimentale' as Flaubert's Mémoire of his Life and Time" (Chicago, University of Chicago).

1944: Wirtz, D. M., "Gustave Flaubert: Pictorial and Plastic Artist" (Madison, University of Wisconsin).

1946: Bonwitt, Marianne, "Flaubert et l'impassibilité" (Berkeley, University of California).

1947: Bart, Benjamin, "Flaubert in Greece" (Cambridge, Harvard University).

1948: Finch, Ilse, "Guide chronologique de la vie de Gustave Flaubert, 1821-1880" (Chicago, University of Chicago).

1949: Carlut, C. E., "Etude sur Flaubert, l'homme, l'artiste, et le penseur avec répertoire critique de la correspondance jusqu'à 1856" (Columbus, Ohio State University).

1949: Congress, Joseph, "Gustave Flaubert and the French Critics, 1857-

1906" (Ithaca, Cornell University).

1949: Cordeu, R. H. "Les jugements littéraires de Gustave Flaubert d'après sa correspondance" (Chicago, University of Chicago).

1950: Gingerich, V. J., "La phrase de Flaubert étudiée dans 'Madame Bovary'" (Iowa City, State University of Iowa).

1950: Runyon, H. J., "Backgrounds and Origins of Realism in the American Novel" (Madison, University of Wisconsin).

1951: Rudich, Norman, "L'unité artistique chez Gustave Flaubert, esthétique rêvée et réelle" (Princeton, Princeton University).

1952: Conn, E. H., "The Impact of 'Madame Bovary' on the English Novel" (New York, Columbia University).

Steisol, M. G., "La phrase de Flaubert étudiée dans 'Salammbô'" (Iowa City, State University of Iowa).

1953: Sachs, Murray, "The Theme of Frustration in the French Novel from Flaubert to Proust (1845-1914)" (New York, Columbia University).

1954: Hoy, M. C., "The Relation of the 'Notes de voyage' to 'Salammbô' and 'Hérodias'" (Bryn Mawr, Bryn Mawr College).

1955: Baker, J. R., "Studies in the Realistic Novel" (Denver, University of Denver).

1955: Smith, H. L., Jr., "The Focus of Narration in the Novels of Gustave Flaubert—an Aspect of his Craft of Fiction" (Madison, University of Wisconsin).

1956: Ramsay, J. A., "The Literary Doctrines of Flaubert, Maupassant and Zola: a Comparative Study" (Urbana, University of Illinois).

1957: Porter, E. G., "Flaubert's Social Attitudes in Relation to his Artistic Theories" (Urbana, University of Illinois).

BIBLIOGRAPHY

PRIMARY SOURCES:
FLAUBERT MATERIALS USED IN THIS STUDY

Flaubert, Gustave, *Œuvres complètes de Gustave Flaubert* (Paris, 1885).
—, *Œuvres de jeunesse inédites* (Paris, 1910).
—, *Correspondance*, 4 vols. (Paris, 1891-1894).
—, *Lettres inédites à Tourgeneff* (Monaco, 1946).
—, *Lettres inédites à Maxime duCamp* (Sceaux, 1948).
—, *Lettres inédites à Raoul-Duval* (Paris, 1950).

SECONDARY SOURCES

Ahlstrom, Anna, *Sur La Langue de Flaubert* (Mâcon, 1899).
Ahnebrink, Lars, *The Beginnings of Naturalism in American Fiction* (Cambridge, Mass., 1950).
Barzun, Jacques, trans,. *A Dictionary of Accepted Ideas* (New York, 1954).
Basler, R. P., *Sex Symbolism and Psychology in Literature* (New Brunswick, N.J., 1948).
Baudelaire, Charles, *L'Art romantique* (Paris, 1923).
Becker, G. J., "Realism: An Essay in Definition", *Modern Language Quarterly*, X (1949), pp. 184-197.
Beer, Thomas, *Stephen Crane* (New York, 1927).
Bergerhoff, E. B. O., "*Réalisme* and Kindred Words: Their Use as Terms of Criticism in the Last Half of the Nineteenth Century", *PMLA*, LIII (1938), pp. 837-843.
Biencourt, Marius, *Une Influence du naturalisme français en Amérique* (Paris, 1933).
Bopp, Léon, *Commentaire sur Madame Bovary* (Neuchâtel, 1951).
Bowers, David, *Foreign Influences in American Life* (Princeton, 1944).
Bowman, J. C., *Contemporary American Criticism* (New York, 1926).
Bowron, Bernard, Jr., "Realism in America", *Comparative Literature*, III (1951), pp. 268-285.
Brawley, A. B., *Attitudes Toward Realism and Science in the "Atlantic Monthly", 1800-1900* (Madison, Wisc., 1955).
Brombert, Victor, *The Criticism of T. S. Eliot* (New Haven, 1949).

130   BIBLIOGRAPHY

Brooks, Van Wyck, *America's Coming of Age* (New York, 1925).
Brown, C. A., *The Achievement of American Criticism* (New York, 1954).
Brown, E. K., *Willa Cather* (New York, 1953).
Buck, Philo, *Literary Criticism* (New York, 1930).
Cabell, J. B., *Beyond Life* (New York, 1930).
Cargill, Oscar, *Intellectual America* (New York, 1941).
Charvat, William, *The Origins of American Critical Thought* (Philadelphia, 1936).
Chase, Richard, *The American Novel and its Tradition* (New York, 1956).
Chinard, Gilbert, "La Littérature française dans le Sud des Etats-Unis", *Revue de la Littérature Comparée*, VIII (1928), p. 87.
Churchill, Allen, *The Improper Bohemians* (New York, 1959).
Colling, Alfred, *Gustave Flaubert* (Paris, 1947).
Cowie, Alexander, *The Rise of the American Novel* (New York, 1948).
Daiches, David, *Critical Approaches to Literature* (Englewood Cliffs, N.J., 1956).
Demorest, D. L., *L'Expression figurée et symbolique dans l'œuvre de Gustave Flaubert* (Paris, 1931).
Descharmes, René, *Autour de Bouvard et Pécuchet* (Paris, 1921).
—, *Flaubert, sa vie, son caractère et ses idées avant 1857* (Paris, 1909).
—, *Gustave Flaubert, sa vie et son œuvre* (Paris, 1909).
Digeon, Claude, *Le Dernier Visage de Flaubert* (Paris, 1946).
DuCamp, Maxime, *Souvenirs littéraires* (Paris, 1906).
Dumesnil, René, *En Marge de Flaubert* (Paris, 1929).
—, *Gustave Flaubert, l'homme et l'œuvre* (Paris, 1932).
—, *L'Education sentimentale de Gustave Flaubert* (Paris, 1936).
—, *La Publication de Madame Bovary* (Paris, 1927).
—, and René Descharmes, *Autour de Flaubert* (Paris, 1912).
Earp, T. W. and G. W. Stonier, *Bouvard et Pécuchet* (Norfolk, Conn., 1954).
Edel, Leon, *The Psychological Novel* (Philadelphia, 1955).
Edwards, Herbert, "Howells and the Controversy Over Realism in American Fiction", *American Literature*, III (November, 1931), pp. 237-248.
—, "Zola and the American Critics", *American Literature*, IV (March, 1932), pp. 114-129.
Emerson, Ralph Waldo, *The Complete Works of Ralph Waldo Emerson* (Boston, 1903).
Everett, A. H., "Literature of Modern Europe", *North American Review*, XXXVIII (1834), p. 158.
Farrel, James T., "A Note on Literary Criticism", *Antioch Review*, I (1936), p. 452.
Fast, Howard, *Literature and Reality* (New York, 1950).
Feidelson, C., and P. Brodkorb, *Interpretations of American Literature* (New York, 1959).
Forster, E. M., *Aspects of the Novel* (New York, 1927).
—, and H. Edwards, "The Impact of French Naturalism on American Critical Opinion", *PMLA*, LXII (September, 1948), pp. 1007-1026.
Garland, Hamlin, *Crumbling Idols* (Chicago, 1894).
Glicksberg, Charles, *American Literary Criticism 1900-1950* (New York, 1951).
Hewlett, M. H., *Last Essays* (London, 1924).
Hoffman, F. J., *The Modern Novel in America* (Chicago, 1956).

—, *The Twenties* (New York, 1955).

Jones, Malcolm, "French Literature and American Criticism, 1870-1900", Ph. D. dissertation, Harvard University (1936).

—, "Criticism of French Fiction in Boston Magazines", *New England Quarterly*, X (1941), p. 488.

Joyaux, G. J., "French Thought in American Magazines". Unpublished Ph. D. dissertation, Michigan State College (1951).

Knight, G. C., *The Critical Period in American Literature* (Chapel Hill, 1951).

La Varende, W., *Flaubert par lui-même* (Paris, 1958).

Levin, H., "What is Realism", *Comparative Literature*, III (1951), pp. 193-199.

MacMahon, Helen, *Criticism of Fiction in the Atlantic Monthly* (Boston, 1938).

Macy, John, "The Spirit of American Literature", *Sewanee Review*, XLIII (1935), p. 175.

Martin, T. J., "The Emergence of the Novel in America — A Study in the Cultural History of an Art Form", Ph. D. dissertation, Ohio State University (1955).

Martino, Pierre, *Le Naturalisme Français* (Paris, 1923).

Mauriac, François, *Trois Grands Hommes devant Dieu* (Paris, 1931).

Morse, J. H., "Schools of Fiction", *Critic*, XXXIII (1915), p. 467.

Mott, F. L., *American Journalism, 1690-1940* (New York, 1941).

—, *Golden Multitudes* (New York, 1947).

—, *A History of American Magazines* (Cambridge, Mass., 1938).

Norris, Frank, *The Responsibility of the Novelist* (New York, 1903).

—, "Responsibilities of the Novel", *Critic*, XLI (1923), p. 537.

O'Conner, W. V., *An Age of Criticism, 1900-1950* (Chicago, 1952).

Parrington, V. L., *The Beginnings of Critical Realism in America* (New York, 1931).

—, *Main Currents in American Thought* (New York, 1941).

Pellew, G., "The New Battle of the Books", *Forum*, V (July, 1888), pp. 391-400.

Pritchard, J. P., *Criticism in America* (Norman, Okla., 1956).

Rabinowitz, A. L., "Criticism of French Novels in American Magazines, 1830-1860", Ph. D. dissertation, Harvard University (1941).

Sainte-Beuve, C., *Causeries du lundi XIII* (Paris, 1912).

—, *Les Nouveaux Lundis IV* (Paris, 1890-1908).

Salvan, A. J., *Zola aux Etats-Unis* (Providence, 1943).

Seillière, E., *Le Romantisme des réalistes* (Paris, 1914).

Smith, B., *Forces in American Criticism* (New York, 1939).

Snell, George, *The Shapers of American Fiction* (New York, 1947).

Spencer, Benjamin, "A National Literature, 1837-1855", *American Literature*, VIII (1936), p. 125.

Spiller, R., *et al.*, *Literary History of the United States* (New York, 1948).

Spingarn, Joel, *Creative Criticism* (New York, 1925).

Suffel, Jacques, *Flaubert* (Paris, 1958).

Thibaudet, Albert, *Gustave Flaubert* (Paris, 1922).

Walcutt, C. C., *American Literary Criticism* (Minneapolis, 1956).

—, "Naturalism in 1946: Dreiser and Farrel", *Accent*, VI (1946), pp. 263-268.

Wellek, René, *A History of Modern Criticism* (New Haven, 1955).

West, R. B., Jr., *Essays in Modern Literary Criticism* (New York, 1952).

Wimsatt, W. and Cleanth Brooks, *Literary Criticism* (New York, 1957).

INDEX